FROM HOME
<small>TO THE</small> **THRONE**

Pauline,

God bless you on
your journey to
the throne!

Tony

FROM HOME
TO THE THRONE

KEYS FOR LIVING FROM THE
STORY OF JOSEPH

TONY WASTALL

LifeSpring PUBLISHING

CONTENTS

ACKNOWLEDGMENTS

I would like to acknowledge the contribution of numerous other people in helping me bring this project to a successful conclusion. In particular I would like to thank Patricia Gray for her meticulous copy editing and constructive advice, Val Hammond for her scrupulous proof reading and helpful suggestions and Paul Airy for crafting my manuscript into a finished book.

I would like to acknowledge the lives of so many friends and mentors who have inspired me through their own heroic journeys to the throne. Finally I would like to thank my wife and best friend Ursula for her selfless encouragement. I dedicate this book to her.

INTRODUCTION

The story of Joseph is five thousand years old yet bang up to date. Everything he experienced – betrayal, injustice, dashed hopes and painful delays – it's no different for men and women today! Haven't you struggled to make sense of life at times? I know I have. Do you ever feel that life has been unfair? Have your dreams been eroded by harsh realities? Joseph had it all, yet none of it stopped him fulfilling the purpose for which he was created.

Born into a dysfunctional family, the youngest of twelve brothers, he was entrusted by God with an incredible dream. Yet everything suddenly turned sour. His jealous siblings stripped him of his clothes and threw him into a pit intending to kill him. Instead they sold Joseph as a slave and he was taken to Egypt. There he ended up serving in the home of Potiphar, captain of Pharaoh's palace guard.

Faithful work for Potiphar was brought to an abrupt end when Joseph refused the advances of his master's wife. Following her false accusations he was thrown into yet another pit, the royal prison.

But Joseph was undeterred. He set about serving in prison and soon found himself in charge. Many years of incarceration passed. But eventually the routine of his grim existence was interrupted. Pharaoh's cup bearer and baker – fellow prisoners who had fallen out of favour with their master, both had dreams that Joseph interpreted. They were released, but once again he was forgotten. Then, as if by the most slender of chances, he found himself thrust before the King in order to interpret dreams that God had planted in the ruler's mind.

From prison, Joseph was catapulted onto a world stage, second only in power to Pharaoh and, ultimately, responsible for saving the kingdom from famine. Finally he was reconciled to his brothers and reunited with his father.

Joseph's story is the stuff of a Hollywood adventure movie! But it's not simply an inspiring rags-to-riches tale. It is recounted with you and me in mind: woven into this amazing narrative are powerful keys and inspiring lessons to help us succeed in life. But more than just succeed in human terms; the story of Joseph is an insight into how God fulfils his cosmic plans through the details and disasters of every day life.

Here we see the bigger picture; how God is at work behind the scenes to position his servant onto the throne of world influence. And God is at work in just the same way today, weaving his awesome purposes through our lives too; the highs and the lows, the good, the bad and as we shall see, the downright ugly!

CHAPTER 1

The Man,
The Message

It is tempting to jump straight into the narrative of Joseph's life; indeed there is so much to unpack. But we will better grasp the deep lessons of his life by stepping back and examining the main character of the story and its context. Let's begin by looking at the book of Genesis itself.

Understanding Genesis

Genesis has been called the seedbed of the bible because its pages refer to every major theme of scripture in embryonic form. From the creation story and the fall of man to the promise of a messiah and the necessity of blood sacrifice, right through to the ultimate destiny of the world, they are all to be found there. But not only does this wonderful book contain the kernel of the entire bible, it provides us with a potted history of mankind. Let me explain:

Genesis opens with a man and woman, Adam and Eve, falling from sonship and fellowship with God. From there we can trace the story through to a man named Abraham and the covenant God made with him. From Abraham comes a family; the children of Israel and from them one particular son – Joseph, chosen by God with a mission to preserve his family and bring salvation to the world. Joseph is rejected by his brothers, suffers terribly, is finally vindicated and raised to the throne of Egypt. Genesis closes with him revealing himself to his brothers and being reconciled to them.

The story of Joseph is what is called a *type*, a symbolic and prophetic shadow of another person. A type points to a greater fulfilment to come. Joseph is a type of Christ. God the Father sent his son to his estranged people the Jews, only to be rejected by them. Although innocent, he suffered shame and reproach at the hands of his 'brothers'. He was taken to the lowest place, death on a cross, and placed in a tomb, where to the natural eye all seemed to end in failure. But God was in total control and raised his son to the throne of heaven. Like Joseph before him, Jesus was lifted up to rescue the world.

So remarkable are the events and details of Joseph's life that some scholars refer to him as the most perfect type of Christ we have in the bible.

But it doesn't end there: Joseph is also a type of us, God's people. Our lives can be overlaid onto this self-same story. You see, God has always had a plan to prepare men and women to reign with him in resurrection power and from that position to bring salvation and blessing to the world. God assured us of this when he originally promised to Abraham, 'through you all the families of the earth shall be blessed' (Genesis 12:3). Joseph was a forerunner of that promise; we the church its ultimate fulfilment.

As with Joseph our road to rule is no walk in the park. It's a path paved with cruel setbacks and injustices. But that is why this account is so important. In Joseph's inspiring story you get to see the picture on the puzzle box of life instead of just the jumble of pieces within! In his life are the map and compass with which you can navigate your own journey. This book is about that journey!

No other bible character quite lives up to Joseph. That great leader Moses got so angry with the people of Israel he was disqualified from entering the land of promise. King David not only committed adultery with Bathsheba but arranged for her husband Uriah to be killed in battle. Elijah the prophet became so depressed he wanted to die. Abraham lied about his wife. Samson was a womaniser – and so we could continue.

I am not suggesting that Joseph was perfect. But his life does demonstrate that a human being living in submission to God can overcome the worst that is thrown at them and still maintain personal integrity and victory. Joseph was vindicated as an ordinary man living in simple trust and belief in his God. In this sense he's no different from you and me! Through Joseph's example, we can all learn to discover the best of God in the worst of whatever life throws at us.

So get ready! We are going to look beneath the surface and find principles in the pages of this story that will liberate your soul and fill you with faith for a future worth living – no matter what you've gone through. But first, we need to look a little more closely at the backdrop to what took place *and* find some keys to interpreting Joseph's life.

Rule, ruin and restoration

One board game my two sons insist on playing with me every

holiday time is 'Risk'. The aim of the game is to conquer the world by defeating countries with your army of plastic soldiers. A single game can last for days but due to the amount of testosterone present in the room I can only endure doses of about an hour at a time! It is no good saying, 'It's just a game!' As far as the boys are concerned this is about world domination and it's a matter of life or death!

The urge to win, the need to take the world by storm, these are in our DNA. We are just wired that way. God made us to rule. But let's be clear exactly what we mean when we refer to 'rule'. We are sometimes uncomfortable with the idea of exercising rule because, from all the evidence mankind has seemed to fail so miserably. The world's problems could be put down to humanity's disastrous attempts at ruling, to its misuse of power.

But that is not the kind of rule God had in mind at all when he created men and women. Rule as God intended is the caring stewardship of creation on God's behalf and for God's purposes. We read about this in Genesis 1:

> *God blessed them and said to them, 'Be fruitful and increase in number; fill the earth and subdue it. Rule over the fish of the sea and the birds of the air and over every living creature that moves on the ground'.*
>
> GENESIS 1:28

The government exercised by Adam and Eve did not come from themselves. It was delegated to them by God, a rule that would bring order, peace and harmony through the whole of creation including human affairs. God purposed that Adam and Eve would produce children and in the course of time populate the earth with his family, a human race living in fellowship with him – with no barriers between heaven and earth.

•

How long this state of harmony existed isn't clear. But for a time Adam and Eve enjoyed unbroken fellowship with God and unthreatened rule over everything he had made. However, God's enemy, Satan, was soon scheming to bring about their downfall and eventually succeeded in tempting them to disobey God.

When Adam and Eve sinned, evil entered their hearts and corrupted every attitude and motivation within them. We call it 'the fall'. It is a good description of what happened. It wasn't that they just slipped up a bit. They lost their former position as God's royal family and co-regents. Their God-given desire to rule became twisted and perverted. Instead of serving their creator, they and their descendants now wanted to be served.

They sought to build empires of their own to satisfy this craving. Power-mad and position-hungry, people were now engaged in a relentless drive for authority and control. That which was meant to exist for the blessing of all creation began working for its destruction. Oppression, warfare and murder are all evidence of a need to dominate everything around.

Amazingly, Adam's fall didn't deflect God from his original purpose. Sin interrupted but did not destroy God's intentions. It simply called forth a plan of restoration. The first step was deliverance from the condemnation brought about by sin. But we shouldn't view salvation from sin as an end in itself. It was the beginning of a process to restore all that he had created back to God's original purpose.

This salvation-plan culminated in the fullness of time, with God sending his son from heaven. Jesus came as God's representative to men and women, to be a provision for our own moral and spiritual bankruptcy. He also came as our representative to God. Jesus is the only human being ever to walk in perfect obedience to God. He not only kept the law but completely fulfilled it and was therefore able to offer himself up to God as a perfect sacrifice for sin.

All that remained was for God to restore for himself a people who would succeed where Adam and Eve failed, and rule once more in the earth. Only in this way will Satan, God's avowed enemy, be completely defeated and humanity be rescued from moral and spiritual famine. Joseph is God's prophetic model for this restoration plan.

Joseph's four homes

There is an important secret to understanding the story of Joseph; it has to do with where he lived. Throughout his life Joseph dwelt in only four homes: his parents' house, that of his master Potiphar, then he progressed to an Egyptian prison and finally, Pharaoh's palace! These four houses signify the four chapters of Joseph's life. They represent the milestones on his journey to the throne, his classrooms in the school of promotion to become governor of Egypt.

To all intents and purposes it seemed as if Joseph was on a downward spiral, from freedom to slavery and ultimately prison, with no hope of escape. But as far as God was concerned his life was completely on track. Nothing was going wrong; he was moving forward in destiny's path.

Joseph began by proving himself faithful in his parents' house. As a mark of success, God promoted him to slavery under Potiphar. When he had made the grade in that house Joseph was moved on to the advanced class in discipleship – the prison! There he passed his exams with distinction and graduated to the palace.

As we consider Joseph's life you'll recognise these houses, for they represent the chapters of life every one of us experience. We all start off in a home of some description. We all experience, to one degree or another, the kind of injustice and rejection that accompanied Joseph in his journey. But none of this is accidental. It is God's way of preparing his people to reign with him.

Unfortunately not everyone makes it to the throne. Some never move beyond the hurdles of home and family. Some submit to the temptations of Potiphar's house. Others succumb to a prison of bitterness and self pity. Graduation is not guaranteed!

Neither is the order we experience these things always identical to Joseph's; sometimes our stay in a particular house is fleeting, at other times it lasts for years! Then there are those baffling times when we seem to revisit a house, where lessons we thought we had already learned are applied all over again.

For Joseph to move on to the next house required him to pass two examinations; they were both 'character papers'. His two tests were in serving and overcoming. In each house he was called to serve a master and overcome an enemy. As he did so God promoted him to the next house.

Joseph's life was supremely marked by these two qualities, serving and overcoming. These two virtues that Joseph modelled are the golden keys to reigning with Christ. Our individual experiences might vary enormously but the keys to the palace remain the same for us all. It is to these keys we now turn our attention.

Joseph the servant

One of the outstanding features of Joseph's life was the way he served in every situation. He began his life helping in his father's house. From there he progressed to Potiphar's house. When he had finished his tour of duty there, God moved him on to the prison where, despite the injustices he faced we find him once again serving. Finally God graduated him to the palace.

But even seated on a throne in Pharaoh's house he didn't stop serving. From the palace he served the whole world. Although he became a mighty ruler, he never ceased to be a servant.

A faithful servant makes the finest sovereign. Joseph was entrusted with the government of the world *because* he was an amazing servant. The greater your ability to serve, the more ready you are to rule. In this respect the kingdom of God stands in absolute contrast to the ways of the world.

In the world you rule others in order to serve yourself
In the kingdom of God you rule yourself in order to serve others

Power in the world is measured by your ability to impose your will on others. The purpose of power in the kingdom of God is to serve others. No one is ready for rule in his realm if they don't know how to serve.

Therefore, promotion is gained through the path of serving. Whatever ministry you exercise and whatever gift you operate, at the end of the day it is all about serving the purpose of God not self-interest. However far you advance in ministry and however great your ambition to be used by God, you will never cease to be a servant. Jesus made this abundantly clear to his own disciples:

> *One day the mother of two of the disciples, James and John, came to Jesus asking for a favour on their behalf. 'Grant that one of these two sons of mine may sit at your right and the other at your left in your kingdom'.*
>
> MATTHEW 20:21

In responding to this request (verse 23), Jesus did not deny that kingly rule was a prospect in the age to come!

'You will indeed drink from my cup, but to sit at my right or left is not for me to grant. These places belong to those for whom they have been prepared by my Father.'

At this, the other disciples joined in the argument over who deserves the best seats in heaven, so Jesus made quite clear just how God's reward system works:

When the ten heard about this, they were indignant with the two brothers. Jesus called them together and said, 'You know that the rulers of the Gentiles lord it over them, and their high officials exercise authority over them. Not so with you. Instead, whoever wants to become great among you must be your servant, and whoever wants to be first must be your slave – just as the Son of Man did not come to be served, but to serve, and to give his life as a ransom for many'.

MATTHEW 20:24-28

Jesus, the lord of all creation said that he came not to be served but to serve and to give his life to save us! The way of the disciple is no different. We are all called to servanthood.

There is yet more we can learn about Joseph's experience as a servant: every house in his life was occupied by a master. Not once did he have the opportunity to choose who that was. It was God's decision every time. So too, we must learn to serve whoever God puts over us. Only then will we be ready for God to take us on to the next house of service.

It is all too easy to become critical and complaining of the person God calls you to serve. But we do not have that luxury. We should honour the one over us with the same spirit as we would wish to be honoured and when God moves us on, we should still honour them. Serving is a form of sowing. If you sow by serving you reap by ruling.

Joseph the overcomer

Joseph was not only a servant; he was also an overcomer. In his first three houses he had to overcome daunting challenges in order to graduate to the fourth house. Overcoming in the first three qualified him to live in the fourth. Overcoming is the way God prepares and qualifies us to rule with him.

> *To him who overcomes, I will give the right to sit with me on my throne, just as I sat down with my father on his throne.*
>
> REVELATION 3:21

The throne is reserved for overcomers. Jesus overcame at the cross and sat at the right hand of his father's throne. Now you and I have the same opportunity to overcome our challenges and win our battles in order to reign with Christ.

Our ability to overcome determines our level of rule

There are things in life that every man and woman *must* overcome if they are to achieve their destiny. It is easy to misinterpret the events and circumstances of life as haphazard and meaningless, but nothing comes to you by chance. God allows many perplexing and difficult circumstances into our lives as opportunities to overcome. Bible teacher Charles Simpson once said, 'The doorway to leadership is protected by many problems'. The sceptre of God will never be tossed around as if in a game of pass-the-parcel for anyone to grab.

Life can be viewed as either an obstacle course or an opportunity course. For the believer the obstacles are no more than opportunities in disguise. It is a sad fact that so many people miss this simple reality and end up resenting what God has allowed for their blessing. The truth of Romans 8:28 must become the bedrock of our lives:

> *And we know that in all things God works for the good of those who love him, who have been called according to his purpose.*

The life of the believer is completely wrapped in the will of God. Every seeming disaster and every perplexing event is an opportunity to grow up, become strong and overcome. Every adversity is God's instrument to confront a fault line of the heart and repair it. How else will God prepare us to reign with him unless we face our inner weakness and frailty? Don't cry, 'Why has this happened to me Lord?' Instead embrace the realities of life head on as God's tools of personal change. As Romans 12:21 challenges us, 'Do not be overcome by evil, but overcome evil with good'.

The word of God contains commands to overcome and promises for all those who do, but it is obvious that not all Christians are overcomers! Overcoming is not an automatic response. It is the school you enrolled in the day you were converted.

Why do we love the Paralympic Games so much? What is the attraction of bravery awards? The answer, I believe, is that people are measured by what they have to overcome in life. Whatever people achieve, the privileges they enjoy or positions they reach in life, it is their response to the handicaps and obstacles they've had to confront that solicits admiration from others.

Every one of us faces a unique set of circumstances in life, challenges tailor-made just for us. None of us has the right to say, 'It's not fair!' We're not judged by our relative starting position in life but by how we deal with the hurdles we face along the way.

The greatest tests we have to overcome are not external but internal, the attitudes and temptations of the heart towards things like hurt, disappointment and delay. The carnal mind is obsessed with overcoming the external circumstances of life. It views people as the enemies of progress and luck as the controlling force. Overcomers like Joseph however, believe their life is in the grip of God. Not once did he view other people as his enemy or himself as the victim of bad luck. He did not seek to beat the system or get his own back on anyone.

Men and women have plenty of ambition and ability to rule the lives of others. Our problems have always been more about taking control of our self, ruling our individual attitudes, our motives and passions. 'Like a city whose walls are broken down, is a man who lacks self-control', says Proverbs 25:28. The greater challenge lies not in imposing your will on others, but in mastering your own thoughts, appetites and desires.

Overcoming takes place in secret. It is when we are on our own that we face our inner enemies. We all like the idea of public victory, of looking good in front of an audience. But the boxing ring of life is rarely surrounded with cheering crowds. It is usually a lonely place.

Public victories are best enjoyed *after* we have learned to gain private victories. David, for example, was only ready to face Goliath when the decisive moment came, because he had already overcome the lion and the bear alone on the hillside.

But David said to Saul, 'Your servant has been keeping
his father's sheep. When a lion or a bear came and carried
off a sheep from the flock, I went after it, struck it and
rescued the sheep from its mouth. When it turned on me,
I seized it by its hair, struck it and killed it. Your servant
has killed both the lion and the bear; this uncircumcised
Philistine will be like one of them, because he has defied
the armies of the living God'.

1 SAMUEL 17:34-36

Out on the hillside David could have thought: 'There's no one
around. No one will miss one lamb. Why should I risk my neck
for that stupid animal?' But he had learned to be faithful guarding
his father's flock and in overcoming his temptations in secret.
Then when it came to facing Goliath in public he didn't buckle
on the inside. Satan could try but he would find no compromise
in him. He had proved God in the secret and private routine of
life; now David was ready for the public arena.

Public victory is only possible when you have learned
private victory in the place where there is no immediate reward
and no one around to praise you. In the place where you are
serving in someone else's house, promoting someone else's cause
or protecting someone else's interests.

Joseph was hand-picked by God for a life's work that
would touch the world in its scope, foreshadow the coming of
the Messiah and live on through history as an example for us to
follow. Let's move on to look inside his first home and see how
this unique life took shape.

For further study

- In what ways are negative thoughts and emotions defeating you? Be honest in facing up to anything you are struggling with and bring it to God right now. Ask him to make the reading of this book a turning point in your life.

- Do you feel thwarted in life by other people or unfair circumstances? If so write down in what ways this is so and hand those things over to God.

- How would you characterise your life – one of serving or of being served? Do you enjoy serving those around you or do you feel you are owed something by others? Try to identify what you feel in answering these questions.

- Read the story of Joseph in Genesis chapters 37-50 in parallel with your reading of this book. Begin now with chapter 37 before going any further.

CHAPTER 2

The Parents' House

Jacob lived in the land where his father had stayed, the land of Canaan. This is the account of Jacob.

Joseph, a young man of seventeen, was tending the flocks with his brothers, the sons of Bilhah and the sons of Zilpah, his father's wives, and he brought their father a bad report about them.

Now Israel loved Joseph more than any of his other sons, because he had been born to him in his old age; and he made a richly ornamented robe for him. When his brothers saw that their father loved him more than any of them, they hated him and could not speak a kind word to him.

GENESIS 37:1-4

Every one of us has a beginning, a home from which our life emerges. Home is the environment that fashions and moulds us at our most formative stage in life.

For some, the thought of home evokes fond memories and pleasant feelings; the security provided by loving parents, family holidays, birthday parties, laughter and fun. For others at the opposite end of the spectrum, memories of home are filled with pain and anxiety; of fighting parents, bullying brothers or sisters, abuse or neglect. The place they should have received love and security became instead a place of torment and mistreatment.

Most of us have tasted a combination of both; the happiest home can be tainted with the sadness of grief, conflict, sickness or trauma. And the harshest of upbringings have rarely been entirely without love from someone such as a grandparent, teacher or neighbour.

Joseph's own home was highly dysfunctional. Although deeply loved by his father, there wasn't much else that could be described as normal. In order to understand the dramatic events that occurred in his early life, let's take a closer look at his family history.

Jacob the father

Joseph's father was Jacob whose very name means 'deceiver.' As a young man Jacob cheated his brother Esau first of his birthright and then his blessing. When things became too hot to handle at home Jacob ran away only to come face to face with God at Bethel. From there he travelled on to his uncle Laban for whom he worked seven years in order to earn his daughter Rachel's hand. When the seven years were up, Jacob himself was tricked and ended up with Rachel's older sister Leah. So he worked yet another seven in order to gain Rachel. Talk about tasting your own medicine!

Joseph was born to Rachel in Jacob's old age. Until that time Rachel had been unable to have children. Leah however produced a total of six sons and a daughter, Dinah, causing a terrible strain between the two women. Things got worse when both of them handed over their servant girls to Jacob to produce even more sons in a perverse kind of competition.

This was the setting Joseph grew up in until tragedy hit. At just eight years of age, he was stricken with grief when his mother Rachel died giving birth to his younger brother Benjamin. Perhaps this explains why his father spoilt him so much! Not long after his mother's death Joseph also witnessed the death of his grandfather Isaac. So already, he was no stranger to grief.

From here on Joseph's home life became a strange and potent environment for a growing boy: he had ten older brothers born to his father by no less than three different women and had to endure the absence of his own mother Rachel. Some children have trouble with one stepmother, but imagine coping with three! Furthermore, his home was filled with smouldering resentment. Rachel had been the favoured wife; now Joseph was the favoured son. His older siblings were consumed with jealousy toward him and had nothing good to say to him. Just to heighten the domestic tension further, another tragedy struck:

> *Israel moved on again and pitched his tent beyond Migdal Eder. While Israel was living in that region, Reuben went in and slept with his father's concubine Bilhah, and Israel heard of it.*
>
> GENESIS 35:21-22

Reuben committed a grave act of betrayal by having sexual relations with Bilhah, the mother of two of his half-brothers. And you thought today's families were complex!

Despite his unusual upbringing, the one constant in Joseph's life was his father's love. Genesis 37:3 says, 'Now Israel loved Joseph more than all his sons, because he was the son of his old age'. Joseph, the favoured son enjoyed a special bond with his father. This passage goes on to say that Joseph's father made a richly ornamented robe for him, the famous 'coat of many colours'. It was this love that formed the bedrock of the boy's life. This was Joseph's home then, crowded with dysfunctional people and twisted relationships. Yet woven through it all was the special tie between father and son.

The father's love

Your experience of an earthly father may not match Joseph's, but one thing we all have in common is God's love. We've all been loved by our heavenly father and this love is the most important truth about our lives. It has made the difference for multitudes of people who would otherwise have been defeated by the experience of their earthly home.

Paul says that God …

> … *chose us in him before the creation of the world to be holy and blameless in his sight. In love he predestined us to be adopted as his sons through Jesus Christ, in accordance with the pleasure of his will.*
>
> EPHESIANS 1:4-5

Whatever home experience you may have endured, it is the love of God that makes your destiny possible. Before you were on the receiving end of any painful experience, God had already reached out to you with his love. You are ultimately defined by this, not merely by your earthly home and family.

The first major secret in life is to discover this love of God yourself. It's the foundation for success, not just one blessing among many that you pick up on the journey. It is the home from which you emerge, 'I will not leave you as orphans I will come to you' (John 14:18), said Jesus, who identified the core need of his disciples as fatherhood. He declared that the Holy Spirit, whose job this is, would communicate this fatherhood to them. It is so much his job that Paul says when he enters the hearts of men and women he cries 'Abba' – the Aramaic word for 'Daddy'. He assures us that we belong to God the father.

This adoption as sons touches every core need we have as human beings. Whatever lack, whatever pain, whatever neglect or abuse, the love of God communicated to us by the Spirit heals and restores us completely. Paul goes so far as to say that, "the love of God has been poured into our hearts by the Holy Spirit who has been given to us." (Romans chapter 5 verse 5).

God is lavish towards us, tipping his love into every crevice of our hearts! This knowledge of the love of God is the bedrock of our lives and knowing that God loves you enables you to trust him in every situation. Bad events will never cause you to doubt it. You will never suppose that God sends sickness to punish you or poverty to watch you suffer. You will always be assured that God is for you, that he watches over you and in him you are secure.

Joseph, the man of destiny

At the age of seventeen Joseph's life was interrupted by a sequence of two dreams:

> *Joseph had a dream, and when he told it to his brothers,*
> *they hated him all the more. He said to them, 'Listen*

to this dream I had: we were binding sheaves of grain
out in the field when suddenly my sheaf rose and stood
upright, while your sheaves gathered around mine and
bowed down to it'.

   His brothers said to him, 'Do you intend to reign
over us? Will you actually rule us?' And they hated him
all the more because of his dream and what he had said.

GENESIS 37:5-8

As if this first dream hadn't stirred up enough trouble, Joseph received a second one and shared that too!

Then he had another dream, and he told it to his brothers.
'Listen', he said, 'I had another dream, and this time the
sun and moon and eleven stars were bowing down to
me'. When he told his father as well as his brothers, his
father rebuked him and said, 'What is this dream you
had? Will your mother and I and your brothers actually
come and bow to the ground before you?'

GENESIS 37:9-10

Revealing these dreams in the way that he did was like lighting the blue touch-paper to his brothers' jealousy, setting in motion the dramatic events of Joseph's life. But first, let us consider the matter of the dreams.

   God placed destiny in the heart of Joseph in the form of his dreams. There is no question that they were supernatural in origin. A seed was planted that would determine his future and the world's salvation. For Joseph those dreams were literal, sudden and obvious in their interpretation.

   Not everyone receives their life-vision in such a dramatic way. Yours may never involve a literal dream at all, nor will it necessarily come suddenly; it may take many years to unfold. But nevertheless, every one of us has been created for a purpose and God longs to communicate that purpose to us in the form of a *vision* or *dream*.

What exactly do we mean by this? A vision or dream is not simply a goal, or ambition. Neither is it the mere product of the imagination. Vision is something buried deep within us. It is not like acquiring a piece of property as you proceed through life. You don't *have* a vision; a vision has you. It is not something you go chasing after but something that comes looking for you, and like Joseph you can often discern its presence as you trace through the path you have come in life.

A dream is the seed of a destiny, an inner conviction tugging away at your heart that you were born for a reason and that your life has a purpose. James Allen in his classic book, *As a Man Thinketh* puts it like this:

> *Your vision is the promise of what you shall one day be. Your ideal is the prophecy of what you shall at last unveil. The greatest achievement was at first and for a time a dream. The oak sleeps in the acorn; the bird waits in the egg; and in the highest vision of the soul a waking angel stirs. Dreams are the seedlings of realities.*

Self-help books and leadership courses often speak about 'developing vision' or 'formulating vision.' But the kind of vision we are referring to here isn't something that can be generated; it is already imprinted on your life. It's woven into the very fabric of your being. You are most likely to find it by looking at what moves you and stirs you within, what you are prepared to give your life to.

Joseph did not invent his dreams; they came from God and were therefore rooted in a divine purpose. It is essential to understand this, because underlying every God-given dream is a God-given cause. Listen to these powerful words:

> *While it is essential to have a vision and to be people of vision, a cause is much more powerful. We talk a lot about vision, destiny and dreams, but it is on the foundation of a cause that vision is birthed. One translation of Proverbs 29:18 says that, 'where there is no progressive revelation, the people perish or die'. A continual unfolding revelation of the cause of Christ will empower any vision and give it purpose. Vision is so much more powerful when it serves a cause.*
>
> BRIAN HOUSTON, FOR THIS CAUSE

A cause is the bedrock of any true God-given dream. It's the reason behind the vision, the spring that gives it life. Beneath Joseph's dream was a cause, the salvation of the world. Initially Joseph was only aware of his dreams. In time he came to realise that his dream served a greater cause. It was an anchor through all the trials of life. Eventually Joseph made it to the palace and saw his visions fulfilled, but he continued to serve the cause for the rest of his life.

If each of us has a God-given vision waiting to be revealed, then indicators of that vision will be evident somewhere now. Don't fall into the trap of waiting for a word to drop out of heaven telling you what God has called you to do in life. It is true that prophecy has its place in confirming what God is forming. But you are more likely to discern God's purpose by digging it up from within your soul. I want to draw your attention to three such indicators of God-given vision.

Passion – People with a God-given dream are moved with a passion – not so much a desire to do something as that deeply felt concern for a cause of which I have already spoken. Every man or woman whom God has used throughout history experienced a burning passion for that thing. Moses felt deeply for the plight of his people bound in slavery even though his own life was secure in the palace. Nehemiah was broken up within when he heard about the state of Jerusalem. Esther was stirred to intercede for her people before the king. What stirs your soul? What makes you cry? What do you feel strongly about? What cause would you give your life for? That's where you will find your dream and locate your vision.

Proficiency – God will gift you for your dream. He will endow you with the qualities you need for all he has called you to do. The mark of the creator is that he equips every living thing for its purpose. So too with your life – he has wired you for the task. It's simply unthinkable that God would stir your heart to do something only to withhold the equipment you need to do it! Just stop and think about your own gifts, aptitudes and abilities. However many or few, God has given you a measure of grace-gifting for the purpose for which he has prepared you.

Positioning – Whatever God has for you will be evident not just internally but externally in the events, circumstances and details of your life. This divine positioning will reveal the path God has prepared for you. God knows how to get you in position for the work he has prepared you for. Look around you and you will see the evidence of God's handiwork. Sometimes it isn't immediately obvious but don't give up. Proverbs 17:4 says, 'the eyes of the fool are in the ends of the earth'. He fails to connect with the reality at the end of his nose! You don't need to chase a dream, just have faith to prosper where you have been planted and you will see the opportunities before you.

All these indicators work together to uniquely prepare us for our destiny. In fact they form our dream, they illustrate our vision. Learn to discern what is already taking place within you rather than running after a spiritual mirage.

Let me illustrate from my own life: I grew up in a Somerset village, miles from the nearest town. The winter of 1963 was particularly harsh and for some weeks our village was cut off by heavy snow falls. I was just eight years old and remember trudging to school with my two sisters through deep drifts. One day a snow plough reached the school and pushed the snow into a long mound at one end of the playground. It must have been fifty feet long, fifteen feet deep and twelve feet high. My friends and I looked up at it in awe!

Then without further ado we began assaulting it. Before long, tunnels and steps began to emerge in the vast heap. I instinctively took charge, assigning tasks to various boys at different points along the mass of snow. In time our vision began to materialise. Each day with shovels and spades we set about our work until a week later we stood back to admire the result; a castle, complete with turrets, battlements, chambers and doorways. Years later I saw the seeds of my destiny in that moment: I would, one day, lead God's people to build God's work!

It took many years for that vision to find its fulfilment. But God was there all along steering my life and causing my destiny to manifest in its time. At the age of seventeen there were no flesh and bones on Joseph's dream, but like a magnet of the heart pulling him forward, his dreams steered him toward God's purpose for his life.

Your dream or inner vision is the most important thing about you. It determines the direction of your whole life. Like Joseph, it will enable you to look beyond the visible world and interpret the circumstances and events of life in the light of what you have seen. Vision is the ultimate governing force of life. Without vision we become prey to the conflicting events around us as we try to make sense of the stuff and nonsense of life.

A dream is essential. It kindles the human spirit with hope and gives meaning to life. David Matthew, in his own book about the life of Joseph puts it like this:

> *Without dreams, the humdrum of life, routine, harsh circumstances and annoying people become unbearable. Men without dreams are prone to nervous breakdowns, bodily sickness and dullness of mind. They have no sense of adventure, no purposeful glint in the eye, no drive.*
> DAVID MATTHEW, DEAD DREAMS CAN LIVE

How about you? What is your dream? What cause do you believe in? Where is your vision? Perhaps your dream has become jaded through hurt and disappointment. Or maybe you have dismissed your dream because you don't feel good enough or qualified enough for it to have come from God!

Sometimes a dream can fade because of long delays and deferred hope. Joseph experienced every kind of attack on his divine dream, yet in the fullness of time God brought it all to fruition. His story is absolutely relevant for us today. God set it in the bible for your encouragement and instruction. It reveals how he works sovereignly in human hearts by first planting dreams in them and then orchestrating their outworking.

Discovering that inner dream is vital in safeguarding your life. Someone has put it this way:

The power to sustain you is the dream within you

Human hope is based on the knowledge of a dream. It creates a sense of future; it nourishes and nurtures your heart. Everyone needs hope and a dream provides it.

The good soil of the heart

It is obvious to me that Joseph did not interpret his dreams as an opportunity to take anything from his family but rather to do them good. God is very careful about who he entrusts a dream of this nature to. I am convinced that Joseph's dreams were pure and were placed by God into a pure heart.

Joseph's only crime, if he had one, was that he shared his dreams! It was this that got him into trouble. Be careful to whom you disclose what God has revealed. Not everyone will be blessed to hear what he is going to do through you. You have to know how to keep a secret with God. Some things must be held in your heart between you and him alone. Talk too soon and you'll live to regret it!

Joseph was a boy with a guileless heart. In his innocence he thought his brothers would be thrilled to hear the dream that they would, one day, bow down before him. He was oblivious to their offence. Some commentators are quick to assume many faults on Joseph's part. I have read descriptions of him as self-righteous, a tell-tale, a show-off and an abuser of God's gift. I struggle with these viewpoints. There is no record of him being rebuked by God for any crime. Neither were the things that happened to Joseph a form of punishment for wrongdoing. Instead we should understand that God entrusted an incredible dream into an innocent and unschooled heart.

I have come to the conclusion that Joseph interpreted his dreams to mean that he would be a source of blessing to his family. But that is not at all how they saw things! His brothers were eaten up with jealousy and the seeds of hatred for Joseph had already been growing in their hearts. Soon these would produce a terrible harvest.

Serving at home

Little is mentioned of Joseph's early home life. But the fragments we do have offer an insight into his servant nature:

> *Joseph, a young man of seventeen, was tending the flocks with his brothers, the sons of Bilhah and the sons of Zilpah, his father's wives.*
>
> GENESIS 37:2

Our first encounter with Joseph finds him serving his father. Joseph was a son but he served in his father's house. The first place we learn to serve is at home, in the setting where God has placed us. In this way we learn to prosper where we have been planted.

> *Now his brothers had gone to graze their father's flocks near Shechem, and Israel said to Joseph, 'As you know, your brothers are grazing the flocks near Shechem. Come, I am going to send you to them'. 'Very well', he replied.*
>
> GENESIS 39:12-13

In the time between these two incidents, Joseph received his supernatural dreams, yet they did not elevate him above serving his father or his brothers. Serving where we have been planted is no threat to our destiny. Serving is the very essence of the will of God. It is the pathway to fulfil your destiny not to jeopardize it.

Despite the awesome glimpses he had received of his destiny to change the world, Joseph was still able to serve those who would one day bow before him.

His father sent him to enquire after the welfare of his brothers. The boy who would become a history-changer not only served those who would one day bow before him, but who would betray him too. He began as an errand boy, serving his brothers and taking messages to them.

Joseph was diligent in his service. When he couldn't find his brothers in Shechem he searched all the way to Dothan. He didn't just serve the letter of his father's instruction but the spirit. This is the mark of a true servant: they seek the satisfaction of the one they serve not themselves. This is the heart that was in Joseph and the heart God is seeking to develop in us his people. It's also the heart that was in Jesus.

> *Even the son of man did not come to be served but to serve, and to give his life as a ransom for many.'*
>
> MARK 10:44

Just like Joseph, Jesus was sent by his father to his 'lost brothers' – to the house of Israel. He came from the heart of God to his own people with the intention of doing them only good. But just like Joseph he was rejected by them. As John records, 'He came to that which was his own but his own did not receive him', (John 1:11).

Jesus left the security of heaven, laid aside his divine glory and stepped down to where we were. He went all the way to his lost people in order to reconcile them to God.

> *When Joseph arrived at Shechem, a man found him wandering in the fields and asked him, 'What are you*

looking for?' He replied, 'I'm looking for my brothers.
Can you tell me where they are grazing their flocks?'
'They have moved on from here', the man answered. 'I
heard them say, "let's go to Dothan"'. So Joseph went after
his brothers and found them near Dothan. But they saw
him in the distance, and before he reached them, they
plotted to kill him.

GENESIS 37:14-18

It is intriguing to read that Joseph found his brothers at Dothan (verse 17) after searching for them at Shechem. Dothan was a place of shame for Jacob's sons. Hamor, the son of the king of Dothan had raped their sister Dinah there and in revenge the sons of Jacob had slaughtered all the men of the city. It was a brutal act of revenge that brought shame on Jacob. It was here that Joseph found them.

In the same way that Joseph had to go all the way to Dothan, so Jesus went all the way to that place of shame for you and me in order to rescue us.

Joseph had no idea what was awaiting him as his brothers caught sight of him in the distance. The damage had already been done in their hearts. Jealousy and hatred were about to spill over in the most spiteful of acts.

For further study

- How would you describe your upbringing? Write a few paragraphs about it. From whom did you receive love as a child? Spend some time thanking God for those people right now and think of some way you can express your gratitude to them if possible.

- Take time to open your heart to God and thank him for loving you. Ask him to pour his love into you in a fresh and powerful way. Allow that experience of his love to cleanse and renew you.

- What God-given dreams do you have? Write them down. At what stage of development are they? Have any of them been frustrated, If so, how? Where would you identify your passion, proficiency and positioning in life?

CHAPTER 3

Betrayed

'Tony, meet Arthur; Arthur meet Tony'. I swung round to the church pew behind me to greet the man I was being introduced to, completely unprepared for what I would see. From the centre of the warm face and friendly smile, two eyes, scarred and blinded, stared back at me. They belonged to Arthur Caiger. I had read about Arthur in the national newspapers, now I had the privilege of meeting him for myself.

Arthur was a probation officer from London and a Christian. On a December night in 1978 he opened his front door to a caller only to receive a face full of acid thrown by a man hidden behind a motorcycle helmet. Arthur recoiled, shrieking in pain as it burnt into his skin. The attacker was one of his probationary clients; someone he had been trying to help. He fled leaving Arthur's family to rush him to hospital. In time his face healed but there was nothing that could be done to save his sight.

That one moment changed Arthur Caiger's life forever. Never again would he be able to look into the faces of his family, enjoy the sights of nature, read a book or travel unaided. An innocent life had been permanently spoiled by a client with a grudge.

How do you handle such a tragedy? Could you ever enjoy life again without being consumed by self pity or anger? In talking to Arthur that evening I was struck by two things; firstly the complete absence of bitterness in him and secondly, in its place, a heart filled with faith. He bore no hatred for the man who robbed him of his sight and he lived with the unshakeable conviction that God loved him and had a purpose for his life that Satan couldn't steal.

Joseph was a man just like that! In one dramatic moment his life was ripped apart for nothing more than a grudge! Yet like Arthur Caiger he walked in forgiveness and love toward those responsible, remaining confident in the goodness of God for an uncertain future. Like Arthur, Joseph was an overcomer!

The pain of rejection

'Here comes that dreamer!' they said to each other. 'Come now, let's kill him and throw him into one of these cisterns and say that a ferocious animal devoured him. Then we'll see what comes of his dreams'.

When Reuben heard this he tried to rescue him from their hands. 'Let's not take his life', he said, 'Don't shed any blood. Throw him into this cistern here in the desert, but don't lay a hand on him'. Reuben said this to rescue him from them and take him back to his father.

GENESIS 37:19-22

As Joseph finally approached his brothers after his long journey, he had little idea of what awaited. Of course they saw him coming and recognised him at once. There was no mistaking that robe! The brothers realised their opportunity to teach him a lesson and immediately began plotting to take his life in the most cowardly way. They were driven by jealousy.

The thing that had really got to them was those dreams. It galled them to think that Joseph should in any way claim authority over them. Now they sensed an opportunity to act and their smouldering resentment was ready to explode. It seems Reuben, the oldest, was the only one who didn't want to go along with the plan:

> *So when Joseph came to his brothers, they stripped him of his robe – the richly ornamented robe he was wearing – and they took him and threw him into the cistern. Now the cistern was empty; there was no water in it. And they sat down to eat their meal. They looked up and saw a caravan of Ishmaelites coming from Gilead. Their camels were loaded with spices, balm and myrrh, and they were on their way to take them down to Egypt.*
>
> GENESIS 37:23-25

Having humiliated Joseph and thrown him into a pit, his siblings sat down to eat and consider their next move. Now it was Judah's turn to intervene and without realising it, become God's instrument for positioning Joseph in Egypt.

> *Judah said to his brothers, 'What will we gain if we kill our brother and cover up his blood? Come, let's sell him to the Ishmaelites and not lay our hands on him; after all, he is our brother, our own flesh and blood'. His*

brothers agreed. So when the Midianite merchants came by, his brothers pulled Joseph out of the cistern and sold him for twenty shekels of silver to the Ishmaelites, who took him to Egypt.

GENESIS 37:23-28

And there it was – problem sorted! They had rid themselves of the object of their spite *and* gained financially in the process!

As we saw in our introduction, in each house that Joseph lived, there was a challenge to overcome. Here in the first house Joseph was given a test in overcoming rejection. It was sudden, brutal and deeply unjust. He experienced the rejection of his brothers.

Like Joseph, the first place we often encounter rejection and mistreatment is on our own door step, among our 'brothers', those closest to us. It is here in 'the parents' house' that we have to learn to overcome hurt from those we should least expect it.

The first recorded murder in human history occurred when a jealous man rose up against his brother; Cain slew Abel because his brother's sacrifice was accepted by God and his wasn't. It seems to have set the pattern doesn't it? Sin spills over into strife as brother is set against brother, or in the words of the prophet, 'A man's enemies are the members of his own household', (Micah 7:6). Ultimately Jesus himself was hounded to the cross by jealous scribes, Pharisees and Jewish leaders – people of his own tribe and tongue.

From within your circle of loved ones, including those closest to you arise conflicts and disputes, jealousy and envy. Have your family or friends rejected you? Have you been the object of a grudge? Are there people who've crossed the road when they saw you coming or haven't spoken to you for years? Wake up! This is reality.

Shock and fear must have gripped Joseph as he found himself wrenched from his father and sold by his own brothers as a slave. Later when recounting what happened, the brothers say, 'truly we are guilty concerning our brother, because we saw the distress of his soul when he pleaded with us, yet we would not listen; therefore this distress has come upon us'. Genesis 42:21. Can you imagine Joseph's desperate cries?

Such acts of rejection are deeply hurtful. They cut the heart with grief and pain, indeed some people never recover. Yet such circumstances don't have the power to destroy you! There are two ways of responding to injustice: you can either behave as a victim or as a victor. You can either see yourself as the helpless target of other people's jealous schemes or view yourself as guided by the sovereign hand of God. In this way nothing need defeat you in life.

Rejection and mistreatment from those we trusted can actually become the tool of God in preparing us for the palace. It's painful, but everyone who God calls to greatness will have to pass through this lesson in overcoming rejection. Jesus said if we want to sit with him on his throne we must first drink from his cup. Resurrection life only follows from the death of self-preservation and self-justification. To be fit for God's use we must first pass through the valley of rejection.

The grace to forgive

None of us are immune from the potential of hurt at the hands of others. I remember some years ago I had passed through a particularly difficult episode with some colleagues. Without realising it I had allowed hardness to enter my heart. I remember one day reading an article in which the American pastor and author R T Kendall was being interviewed. One of the questions he was asked particularly intrigued me: What is your life's motto? 'How interesting', I thought, totally unaware that God was setting me up! The words that followed pierced me like an arrow: 'Total forgiveness, however deep the hurt'. I just broke down immediately. Tears flowed from my eyes as I forgave my brothers and asked God to forgive me for my hardness of heart.

There will always be a need for forgiveness in your own home. A husband will need to forgive his wife; a wife likewise her husband. Parents will need to forgive children and, hard though it might be, children their parents. Siblings will need to forgive each other as will friends, fellow leaders, church members, neighbours and workmates.

God spoke to me through an unusual scripture at the time of this incident in my life. In Zechariah 13 we read how the prophets would one day deny their ministry for fear of persecution from a backslidden people. They would be put on the spot by suspicious people:

> *And one will say to him, 'what are these wounds between your arms?' Then he will say, 'Those with which I was wounded in the house of my friends'.*
>
> ZECHARIAH 13:6

No-one's suspicions would be raised by such a reply because everyone apparently accepted that it was normal to get hurt in the house of those you are close to! The nearer you are to a group of people, the greater the potential for hurt and offence.

I watch some Christians, for example, roam from church to church on a three to five year cycle. First comes the honeymoon period when the pastor can do no wrong and the church seems made in heaven. Then comes the settling down period before the cracks appear. It is then only a matter of time before offences accumulate and recriminations follow.

The saga ends with them resigning in disillusionment to continue their search elsewhere for the perfect church. But it doesn't matter where you go to get away from people; the one person you will always bump into is yourself!

It is clear that Joseph overcame the offence he suffered at the hands of his brothers before he moved on to Potiphar's house. He did not drag it around with him. He did not have to return to this episode at some future stage of life in order to get his attitude sorted out. His forgiveness is a model for us.

Three things strike me about Joseph's forgiveness of his brothers. First he forgave them immediately! Forgiveness must be given at the time of the offence. It is clear this is how Joseph forgave, for he would not have been able to serve as he did or live in faith if resentment had still been smouldering in his heart.

Then he forgave them completely. There was no remnant of bitterness left in Joseph's heart to rise up at some future date and spoil his victory. Forgiveness that is selective is not forgiveness at all!

Finally he forgave them freely. Forgiveness must never be conditional on something or someone else. Jesus taught us that we should forgive regardless of the guilty party's response – or lack of it. His forgiveness was unconditional and ours must be too.

Forgiveness is essential! Joseph learned to forgive early on in life. He didn't allow a root of bitterness to establish itself in his heart. He was not haunted or taunted by the malicious act of his brothers.

The only remedy to hurt and offence is total forgiveness. Jesus himself left us no other option. On one occasion he told a parable about a servant who owed his master the king ten thousand talents – a vast sum in today's money! The servant begged for mercy and the king responded by cancelling his debt.

But on his way out the same man bumped into a fellow servant who owed him just pocket change. He immediately demanded to be repaid:

> *The servant fell to his knees and begged him, 'Be patient with me and I will pay you back'. But he refused. Instead, he went off and had the man thrown onto prison until he could pay the debt. When the other servants saw what had happened, they were greatly distressed and went and told their master everything that had happened.*
>
> *Then the master called the servant in. 'You wicked servant', he said, 'I cancelled all that debt of yours because you begged me to. Shouldn't you have had mercy on your fellow servant just as I had on you?' In anger his master turned him over to the jailers to be tortured, until he should pay back all he owed.*
>
> *This is how my heavenly father will treat each of you unless you forgive your brother from your heart.*
>
> MATTHEW 18:26-35

The person who forgives is free! The one who harbours a grudge is cast by God into a prison. What should we make of the reference to torturers? Unforgiving people are racked by a host of mental and emotional torments. The need to get even, frustration and anger; all these plague the heart of the resentful. The only escape to peace is the grace of God. As God in Christ forgave us so too we must forgive.

The stumbling block that holds many back from doing so is the galling sense of injustice they feel; the perpetrator seems to get away scot-free while the victim often continues to suffer.

Not so! Forgiveness is the doorway through which the healing love of God flows toward the one who has suffered. Once that door has been opened there's no limit to what the restoring and transforming grace of God can accomplish.

On the other hand, no one who violates the laws of God, who inflicts hurt or commits crime against another human being, is free unless they too come to the cross of Christ for mercy and forgiveness. Forget appearances; the perpetrator of pain has gained nothing, least of all escape from the justice of God.

Have you been hurt by someone? Undoubtedly! Have you forgiven that person? If there is any doubt, make it the supreme priority of your life to rid your heart of every scrap of anger, bitterness and resentment.

The forgiveness that Joseph displayed became a foundation of his future, for he was about to face even worse treatment and greater reason for offence, but he faced them as a free person! For if unforgiveness is allowed to lodge in the heart, it pollutes the whole being. 'It's not fair!' becomes our automatic response to everything life flings at us and our personality gets corroded with resentment. Those who forgive however, quickly learn to walk in forgiveness and find their heart strengthened for all the many assaults of life.

Wrapped in his will

Joseph graduated from his first class in discipleship at a young age! But it is tragic that there are so many believers who have gone through life never having overcome in the God-sent opportunities they encountered early on. They stumbled over the rock of offence and struggled to forgive. They allowed their heart to be poisoned with bitterness and failed to see the hand of a loving God behind the seemingly random events of their life.

I once prayed with a man in his seventies who had not spoken to his son for thirty-four years simply because he could not let go of an offence. This man wept tears of remorse the like I have rarely seen as he faced up to the pride that had robbed him of decades of relationship with his son, his daughter in law and the grandchildren he had never met.

Joseph kept his heart clear of offence. He could have been completely overwhelmed by hatred and the desire for vengeance. But he was governed by something much greater. The thing that protected Joseph was the knowledge that he was wrapped in the will of God.

When Reuben returned to the cistern and saw that Joseph was not there, he tore his clothes. He went back to his brothers and said, 'The boy isn't there. Where can I turn now?' Then they got Joseph's robe, slaughtered a goat and dipped the robe into the blood. They took the ornamented robe back to their father and said, 'We found this. Examine it to see whether it is your son's robe.'

He recognised it and said, 'It is my son's robe! Some ferocious animal has devoured him. Joseph has surely been torn to pieces'.

GENESIS 37:29-33

Joseph must have realised that Jacob too would suffer through this episode. But he was powerless to do anything for the father he loved. If his brothers were prepared to go to such lengths to satisfy their grudge, what would they now say to their father to protect their evil scheme?

It is impossible to contain sin. It spills out to affect others. When one person is hurt, others will resonate with that hurt. One offence will multiply as other people are caught up in the wake of the wrongdoing. Joseph had no option but to trust God for the people for whom he could do nothing, most of all, his father.

> *Then Jacob tore his clothes, put on sack-cloth and mourned*
> *for his son many days. All his sons and daughters came to*
> *comfort him, but he refused to be comforted, 'No', he said,*
> *'in mourning will I go down to the grave to my son'. So*
> *his father wept for him. Meanwhile, the Midianites sold*
> *Joseph in Egypt to Potiphar, one of Pharaoh's officials,*
> *the captain of the guard.*
>
> GENESIS 37:34-36

Despite the terrible crime the brothers had commited; there is some irony in the contrasting responses of Joseph and his father. Without questioning the evidence or plausibility of the report, old Jacob swallowed the lie of his son's apparent death, hook line and sinker and slumped into mourning. Joseph on the other hand, put his trust in God and stayed at peace in his heart, when he was the one who actually had the most to endure!

Jacob was trapped in unbelief. A negative, pessimistic old man, he didn't enquire with God, but resigned himself to believe the worst for Joseph, and so endured much of his old age in morbid and unnecessary grief. Jacob was defeated because he abandoned his dream, but thankfully as we will see, this wasn't the end of his story. Joseph, on the other hand, was sustained because he held onto his dream.

It is not easy to remain in faith when those around you react with doubt, fear or unbelief. But you cannot afford to be swayed by them. Never let go your *victory* in God just because others are not enjoying *their* victory. You will never help a person by joining them in their problem! Joseph could do nothing to help his father. He knew Jacob would be in anguish. But the best way to help his father was to continue to trust in God himself, and not allow worry to dominate his future.

What a mess! Tragedy had engulfed this family. Yet God was not far away, he was fulfilling an incredible plan through each twist and turn. Now Joseph was launched into his adventure, sent ahead by God to Egypt in the most unlikely of ways. What his brothers intended for harm, in time they would all see, God intended for good ... for the saving of many lives (Genesis 50:19).

For further study

- In this chapter we examined Joseph's first great test, rejection and betrayal by family members. Have you experienced something like this in life? How has it affected you? Take time to forgive anyone who has hurt or offended you. Name them before God and release them to him.

- Now face the prospect that you have mistreated others. As someone once said, 'Hurt people hurt people!' Ask God to show you how this may be applicable and receive his forgiveness through repentance and confession of your sin. Then open up to the grace of God and allow his love into those raw areas of your personality.

- Evaluate your relationships and friendships in the light of this chapter. Identify good relationships that genuinely strengthen and encourage you. Thank God for them and seek ways to bless these people. Then identify negative and dysfunctional relationships. Let God adjust these, pruning where necessary so they are not dictating your life.

CHAPTER 4

Potiphar's House

On 20th December 1974, Chris Carrier a boy just ten years of age from Southern Florida was abducted by a former employee of his father. The sacked worker had hatched the ultimate plan to get even. He would kill his former employer's son!

Walking home from school that fateful day, Chris was approached by a man claiming to be a friend of his father. Would Chris help him prepare a Christmas party for his Dad? Agreeing to help, Chris went with the man on what he thought was a shopping trip to a nearby store. Instead he was driven into the Florida Everglades where he was attacked with a pickaxe.

Then forced out of the car and into the undergrowth, he was shot in the head and left for dead. Six days later Chris was found by a man out deer hunting. Incredibly he was alive. The bullet had passed straight through his skull and despite being blinded in one eye he suffered no permanent brain damage.

Over the intervening months Chris Carrier struggled to come to terms with what his attacker had done. He could no longer participate in contact sports, his vision was impaired and he was self-conscious about his appearance. The attack had also left him emotionally scarred as he battled with confusion and resentment.

But at the age of thirteen a remarkable change occurred. Chris realised he could not remain angry forever. His injuries could have been far worse; he could easily have been killed! He made the decision to turn from self-pity and the desire for revenge forever and by so doing began to live again.

Twenty-two years passed, when out of the blue Chris received a phone call that would once again change his life. The police were calling to notify him that a man by the name of David McAllister had confessed to being his abductor. Chris visited David McAllister the following day. He described what happened this way:

> *When I visited him that afternoon, I felt an overwhelming compassion for the man. David McAllister was no longer an intimidating abductor. He was, instead, a frail seventy-seven year old who weighed little more than sixty pounds. Glaucoma had left him blind, and his body had been ruined by alcoholism and smoking. He had no family or friends. He was a man who faced death with only his regrets to keep him company.*
>
> *When I first spoke to David, he was rather callous. I suppose he thought I was another police officer. A friend who had accompanied me wisely asked him a few simple questions that led to him admitting that he had abducted me. He then asked, 'Did you ever wish you could tell that young boy that you were sorry for what you did?' David answered emphatically, 'I wish I could.'*
>
> *That was when I introduced myself to him.*

*Unable to see, he clasped my hand and told me he was
sorry for what he had done to me. In return, I offered
him my forgiveness and friendship.*

Chris was not only able to face his attacker but befriend and
help him because he had already forgiven him. In the days that
followed, he visited the old man regularly, often with his wife
and two daughters. As they talked, his hardness gradually melted
away. Then one evening just three weeks later, David McAllister
passed away. Chris Carrier, his new-found friend was at his side.
Chris goes on to say:

> *There is a very pragmatic reason for forgiving. When we
> are wronged, we can either respond by seeking revenge,
> or we can forgive. If we choose revenge our lives will be
> consumed by anger. When vengeance is served it leaves
> us empty. Anger is a hard urge to satisfy and can become
> habitual. But forgiveness allows us to move on.*
>
> *There is also a more compelling reason to forgive.
> Forgiveness is a gift – it is mercy. It is a gift that I have
> received and also given away. In both cases, it has been
> completely satisfying.*

An innocent life snatched away because of a grudge! Like Joseph,
Chris Carrier was deeply marked by his suffering and confusion.
But also like Joseph it was not the end. What began so tragically
found a remarkable fulfilment many years later with forgiveness
and friendship for the man who had committed the wrong.
Chris revealed himself to his attacker and rescued him just as
Joseph revealed himself to his brothers and rescued them.

It was made possible because a door to the future had
been opened through forgiveness. Chris Carrier learned that

you can't enjoy the future until you let go of the past! It was the same for Joseph. He was now entering a new house; but it was a promotion not a setback. He had no idea what lay ahead, just the knowledge that his God was with him.

The Lord was with Joseph

> *Now Joseph had been taken down to Egypt. Potiphar, an Egyptian who was one of Pharaoh's officials, the captain of the guard, bought him from the Ishmaelites who had taken him there.*
>
> GENESIS 39:1

Put yourself in Joseph's shoes for a moment and try to appreciate how he felt at this point in time. In the space of a few days he had been completely severed from his family and home. Betrayed by his own brothers and sold as a slave into Egypt, he found himself utterly alone and completely powerless. Lashed with a whip, shouted at in a strange tongue, thirsty and tired, Joseph faced a perilous future.

No doubt because of his youthfulness, fitness and health, Joseph caught the eye of one of Egypt's leading men – Potiphar the captain of Pharaoh's guard. Money quickly changed hands.

The description of Potiphar as 'captain of the guard' literally means 'captain of the executioners' – the commanding officer of the royal body-guard responsible for capital sentences ordered by the king. Talk about out of the frying pan and into the fire! Serving this man as a member of his household, Joseph was now perfectly positioned by God for the next phase of preparation for the throne.

Genesis 39:2 makes the comment, 'the Lord was with Joseph and he prospered, and he lived in the house of his

Egyptian master'. At face value this is a difficult statement to grasp. How could God be with Joseph when he has not only been betrayed by his brothers but sold as a slave into Egypt? The truth is, however, that you can't gauge the presence of God by the favourability of your circumstances.

In reality, nothing had taken place that could separate Joseph from God's presence. As F B Meyer says in his biography of Joseph, 'The only thing that separates us from God is sin'. But Joseph's character was blameless. He was living in forgiveness toward his brothers and faith toward God for his future. God was with him!

At this point the only thing Joseph had left to hold onto was the presence of God; everything else was gone. He had been stripped of his cloak but not his God. His jealous brothers could not peel the favour of God away from him and, thankfully, this was the only thing that counted!

It doesn't matter how people treat you and what they do to you, no one can take the presence of God away from you. But that's OK, because it is the presence of God not favourable circumstances that guarantees your future.

When Genesis says, 'The Lord was with Joseph', it means his divine favour, his active grace. It means God was watching over him, protecting him and guiding his ways. Genesis 39:4 also says that, 'Joseph found favour'. He attracted the favour of God because he walked in his ways. Goodness and mercy followed Joseph because he kept his heart clear with God.

There is no success in life without God's favour. But favour is not something you chase after, it chases after you! The word of God shows us that favour is a fruit. It grows on the branches of a life that attracts God's pleasure. Notice what else God's word has to say about this:

- You bless the righteous; you surround them with favour as with a shield. Psalm 5:12

- He who seeks good finds favour. Proverbs 11:27

- A good man will obtain favour from the Lord. Proverbs 12:2

- Favour is found among the upright. Proverbs 14:9

God's favour is not restricted to ideal circumstances. You can find it in unfavourable situations because favour comes from heaven not earth. Genesis goes on to say that Joseph prospered in Potiphar's house. Prosperity was how God's favour was manifest to Joseph. Although he was betrayed by his brothers and sold as a slave, none of this prevented him from prospering because his success originated in God, not man.

Serving as a slave

> *When his master saw that the Lord was with him and that the Lord gave him success in everything he did, Joseph found favour in his eyes and became his attendant.*
>
> Genesis 39:3-4

Joseph had served faithfully in the house of his father. He had overcome the callous action of his brothers. Now he was re-positioned by God for a new level of living. It may look like a bit of a come-down to you and me but it was a step up as far as God was concerned. Joseph's promotion follows a simple principle.

In the kingdom of God, reward takes the form of more responsibility

Joseph's move to the house of Potiphar was a reward for his faithfulness. His new job description would require more of him more grace, more virtue, more trust and more faith. Every time we are promoted to a new house, there are new challenges. Have you ever played those computer games where you move from level to level by fighting off some enemy? Have you noticed that the higher you go the more challenging it gets? The same principal is at stake here: for every new level there is a new devil.

Jesus taught this principle in one of his parables regarding the age to come:

> *A man of noble birth went to a distant country to have himself appointed king and then to return. So he called ten of his servants and gave them ten minas. 'Put this money to work, he said, 'until I come back'. But his subjects hated him and sent a delegation after him to say, 'We don't want this man to be our king'.*
>
> *He was made king however, and returned home. Then he sent for the servants to whom he had given the money, in order to find out what they had gained from it. The first one came and said, 'Sir, your mina has earned ten more'. 'Well done, my good servant!' his master replied. 'Because you have been trustworthy in a very small matter, take charge of ten cities'.*
>
> LUKE 19:12-17

The servant was rewarded for his faithfulness with something much more challenging than looking after some cash – the government of ten cities! Now Joseph was facing fresh challenges, a new level of lessons to be learned and he was serving not as a son but as a slave.

Remarkably, despite his position, he served as if he were a free man with a free heart. This was Joseph's choice, despite his status as a slave.

Under Potiphar, he learned to serve in another man's house and did the very best job he could, even though he knew he would have no inheritance in this house. He would never be a son here. He would only ever be a slave. He would never own or receive anything in this house. The only beneficiary of Joseph's work would be the one he served – Potiphar.

Under the jurisdiction of Pharaoh's Captain of the Guard, God dealt with the issue of ownership in the heart of his servant. Joseph owned nothing yet he served with the same care and diligence as if everything was his. He was as careful with another man's house as he would be with his own.

The truth is we never actually own anything in life. Everything that comes our way is a stewardship from God. But the problem is so many of God's people behave as if they are the owners. You hear the language of ownership all the time: 'my church, my ministry, my money, and my people'.

This attitude of ownership is a curse in the church today and a constant frustration to God's will being done. Ownership lies at the root of power struggles and church politics. Ownership corrupts leaders in their handling of money. Ownership seeks to control people instead of promoting them, to use people rather than serve them.

There is only room for one owner in the church and that is Jesus. He is the head of his body, the architect of the house, the king of the kingdom. Paul said to the elders of Ephesus, 'Be shepherds of the church of God which he bought with his own blood', (Acts 20:28). Leaders might be shepherds and care-takers but Jesus is the owner! The church has already been paid for with his blood – there isn't room for any other owner. Ministers do not own ministries. Apostles do not own churches. Pastors do not own congregations – God does!

> *Potiphar put him in charge of his household, and he entrusted to his care everything he owned. From the time he put him in charge of his household and of all that he owned, the Lord blessed the household of the Egyptian because of Joseph. The blessing of the Lord was on everything Potiphar had, both in the house and the field.*
>
> GENESIS 39:4-5

Joseph was promoted because he served Potiphar as though he were serving God. He didn't seek promotion he sought the good of his master and God promoted him, because promotion comes from God.

It does not always work out this way. For instance King David suffered at the hands of his own son Absalom who rose up to overthrow his father; see 1 Samuel 15. This 'Absalom spirit' stands in complete contrast to that of Joseph. Tragically it's still at work today. What does it look like?

• Absalom is never satisfied with what he has. No matter how much he is given he always wants more. At the root of it all is a sense that he is not being treated fairly.

• Absalom uses his father's house to build his own following. All the time he is harbouring an agenda of his own.

- Absalom is ruthless and vengeful. When David had served his useful purpose, Absalom had no problem dispensing with him. A true son is devoted to the house of his father but Absalom is only interested in what he can grab.

God knows how to promote you when you are faithful in your stewardship. It will not come through grabbing a position or gained by flattery or deception. Promotion is received by laying down your life for the interests of those you serve.

God wants you to serve another person when there is no prospect of reward. He wants you to serve whether you are promoted or passed over, recognised or replaced. We are not ready for palace rule until we are prepared to live and serve in the house of Potiphar for as long as God wants. God cannot entrust you with your own house until you have learned to serve in the house of another.

Don't ever be guilty of an attitude that says, 'I am owed a position'. The greatest title we could ever aspire to is that of 'Servant of God'. This should be enough.

A word of caution is in order here: Joseph was being held against his will. He was not enjoying this experience of slavery. He did not relish his restriction. But he was confident that God was in control and that this house was not permanent. We must stay when God says stay and move when he says move. Never allow yourself to be manipulated by someone into serving them rather than God.

From God, Potiphar received the benefits of Joseph's service. God blessed an idol worshipping Egyptian because of the presence of a covenant man. Joseph behaved as a steward and this attitude of stewardship released blessing into his life. When we serve freely, God is able to bless us in spite of our circumstances.

So he left in Joseph's care everything he had; with Joseph in charge, he did not concern himself with anything except the food he ate.

Genesis 39:6

Joseph coveted nothing in Potiphar's house. He wasn't jealous of his riches and didn't begrudge Potiphar any of the benefits that came his owner's way as a consequence of the blessing that rested upon his own life. A relationship of absolute trust had developed between Potiphar and Joseph because Joseph served him as if he were a true son.

Joseph is a model of an attitude God is determined to breed in his people. He is raising up a generation whose aim is to promote the body of Christ and the interests of God. Our service should never be given because of a need for recognition or to fulfil frustrated ambition but out of devotion to the Lord wherever he places you.

Whatever your hand finds to do

Whatever your hand finds to do, do it with all your might.

Ecclesiastes 9:10

Joseph was taken to the house of Potiphar against his will. Yet he served there with all his heart. He could exercise no choices of his own under Potiphar. As a slave he was told exactly what to do. He was denied all freedom.

There are times in life when only one door seems to open before you. As soon as you walk through that door, the path to God's greater purpose opens up to you. The activity at hand might not be the ultimate thing he has in mind, but it leads you further into his purposes for you.

At the time when my wife and I finished studying at Bible School we had no idea what we would be doing next. Our first child was due in four months and all we knew was that we should move to a certain city. I desperately wanted a full time ministry opportunity to open up but it was not the right time. So I urgently set about job hunting. Unfortunately only one vacancy opened up for me and that didn't look too promising!

It was the position of salesman for a specialist electrical company. The salary was poor and the office was a long drive away from home. I had no sales experience. The company was in decline! To the outward appearance it was far from ideal, but I felt strongly to accept the position. I took the one door that opened to me and found the grace of God was waiting for me there.

At that point I determined this would be my finest hour. I would work here with the best of my ability 'as unto the Lord'. I would do what my hand found to do with all my strength.

You must always begin with what is before you. The hardest thing at times is to recognise the grace of God in the thing at hand. When God sent Elisha to help a destitute widow he asked her, 'What do you have in your house?' She replied, 'Your servant has nothing there at all except a little oil', (2 Kings 4:2). But this so-called 'nothing' was in fact the key to her miracle. It was all God needed. When she presented it to Elisha God multiplied that oil in the vessels she brought him.

I found to my joy, that God was with me in that job and I prospered. Not only so, the company prospered too. Within eighteen months I was offered the position of UK Sales Manager. I actually turned the promotion down because God was moving me from that house to the ministry for which I had waited so long.

It is the easiest thing to overlook the obvious, to discount the insignificant, and reject the objectionable. But God's will embraces all of those things. Don't have your head in the clouds and miss what is at your feet! What opportunities have you passed over because they came disguised as delays or inconveniences? Everything in life is an opportunity for the man or woman who genuinely seeks God's will. Don't reject them. Embrace what is before you and see how God will open up new paths for your life.

For further study

- What stewardship has God placed into your life? By that I mean responsibility, gifting, or area of serving. What about your job, family, finances or possessions? Thank God for them and determine to be a faithful steward of everything he has entrusted to you.

- Have you left any church or friendship situation in bad attitude or with unresolved baggage? Ask God to forgive you and if possible seek the forgiveness of anyone you have wronged.

- Now read Genesis 39 before going any further.

CHAPTER 5

The Price of Integrity

Life was not all bad now! Although still a slave, Joseph had become a man of influence and status. God had prospered him; he was entrusted with everything in his master's house and would have enjoyed considerable benefits as a senior servant. Yet at this precise moment Joseph faced his most dangerous threat: his master's wife tried to seduce him.

> *Now Joseph was well-built and handsome, and after a while his master's wife took notice of Joseph and said, 'Come to bed with me'.*
>
> GENESIS 39:6-7

Overcoming in Potiphar's house

In Potiphar's house, Joseph had to overcome temptation – sexual temptation in particular. Joseph was put right in the line of fire. This was not some little distraction he had to swat away. It was in-your-face, full-on, sustained assault!

The injustice of this young man's situation is brought into sharp relief when Potiphar's wife attempts to seduce him. Here's Joseph unjustly separated from his family and held against his will. Despite his success with Potiphar he was still no more than a slave. Yet he had maintained a good heart and served with grace. Joseph could so easily have pandered to his flesh here; comforted himself with a little sexual gratification and justified it afterwards because of all he had suffered. 'Surely God would excuse me for just one indulgence?'

But Joseph overcame sexual temptation not just once but over a sustained period. Genesis 39:10 puts it this way, 'And though she spoke to Joseph day after day, he refused to go to bed with her or even be with her'.

Nowadays it's common to hear people from all walks of life seek to justify sexual immorality as natural and inevitable, 'You can't help it. We're all human. Sex is just a physical need. No point in getting hung up about it.' Such an attitude promotes the lies that sexual sin is either excusable or no sin at all. We all have the ability to choose and we always have the power to say 'no!' Joseph proves that it is possible. He overcame the flesh in the harshest of circumstances:

> But he refused. 'With me in charge', he told her, 'my master does not concern himself with anything in the house; everything he owns he has entrusted to my care. No one is greater in this house than I am. My master has withheld nothing from me except you, because you are his wife. How then could I do such a wicked thing and sin against God?"
>
> GENESIS 39:8-9

Joseph lacked the encouragement and support of friends.

He was denied the legitimate outlet of sexual drive within marriage. He didn't have a church or own a bible to draw strength from. He didn't manage to walk away from temptation because the circumstances were easy; but overcame through personal integrity.

It wasn't the fear of punishment that made Joseph refuse Potiphar's wife. It wasn't because she was unattractive or he had a better offer. He said 'no' because it was wrong on two counts:

Firstly, it would have been a betrayal of his master. As he declared, 'my master does not concern himself with anything in the house'. He would not betray that trust. Secondly, it would have been a sin against his Maker. Joseph goes on to say, 'how could I do such a wicked thing against God?'

No, Joseph refused because he was a man of integrity and principle. He defeated sexual sin because he lived a life established on God's standards of righteousness and justice, of loyalty and honour. This is the only way to overcome any kind of sin. Psalm 25:21 says, 'May integrity and uprightness protect me'.

Integrity means wholeness. It comes from the Latin word *integer* meaning one. It means your life is the same all the way through. Like a stick of seaside rock, wherever you break it, you find the same message. The only safeguard against sin is a moral foundation of integrity in your life. Anything less will not read true.

Genesis 39:10 says that, 'she spoke to Joseph day after day'. This was no one-off enticement. She bugged him constantly in an unremitting attempt to wear him down. We must understand that overcoming sin is a daily issue of walking with God. Temptation never takes a holiday. It will never give up. It is conquered through vigilance; by maintaining active fellowship with God and by obeying the Holy Spirit every day.

Verse 10 goes on to say that, 'Joseph would not even be alone with her'. He deliberately avoided the place of temptation and protected himself by putting distance between him and the problem! Joseph did not view Potiphar's wife as a friend or confidant. He did not let her flirt with him. He didn't chase her face down the canyons of his mind. He didn't indulge in thinking 'what might have been' if they had met in another set of circumstances.

Joseph is not the only man to have overcome such intense testing. Hebrews 4:15 says that, 'Jesus was also tempted in every way that we are, yet without sinning'. Jesus overcame temptation as a man living in submission to God. He did not play the 'I'm the son of God' card to gain an advantage over the rest of us. The secret of his freedom was the fear of God – just as it is for us. Jesus loved righteousness and hated wickedness; he walked in daily obedience to his father and so maintained his integrity.

Generation XXX

Men and women of God today must overcome sexual temptation. As I look back on many years as a believer and in ministry I shudder to think of the number of people I know who have fallen into sexual sin. Sadly, the damage is never confined; each occasion is a cause of hurt and injury to others. Without doubt every one of us will experience sexual temptation in life so let me say this loud and clear, we must learn to confront and overcome it. It cannot be buried, excused, ignored or trivialised.

Today, opportunities to commit sexual sin have exploded. In the internet age in which we live the most graphic pornography is just three clicks away. It is estimated that 70 per cent of internet use is to access sex sites. Add to this the easily available magazines, tabloid newspapers, telephone chat lines, cable television and sex clubs and you can see that we are besieged by sexual temptation on every side.

Sadly it would seem that Christian leaders are no less vulnerable. A recent survey of ministers for example, revealed that 40 per cent of those questioned confessed to having been tempted with internet pornography.

When leaders do fall morally the damage is all the greater. It is not just the immediate family that suffers but the body of Christ that is injured and the name of Christ that becomes a reproach in the world. As Zechariah 13:7 warns, 'Strike the shepherd and the sheep will be scattered'. Satan knows if he can defeat spiritual leaders, the people in their care will also suffer and the house of God be fragmented.

Much sexual sin today is invisible to others, it takes place behind closed doors in a secret fantasy world from where it develops into a moral cancer weakening and compromising the effectiveness of the church and its leaders. I appeal for you to heed Paul's advice in 1 Corinthians 10:12, 'So if you think you are standing firm, be careful that you don't fall'. No one is immune to sexual temptation, least of all those who think they are beyond its reach.

I am often asked the question, 'What about those who have already fallen? Is there any hope?' Thank God for his amazing grace. There is forgiveness and restoration for those who have given way to sexual sin. The story of David is a case in point. He committed adultery with Bathsheba and then, to compound this evil, had her innocent husband Uriah killed. Yet God demonstrated his amazing grace and mercy to him in response to his repentance.

If you have fallen morally in any way don't sweep it under the carpet of your life. Get right with God and seek help from a trusted leader. Take advantage of the grace and forgiveness that is in Jesus Christ. Our God is able to restore you and remove the scars that remain from falling.

This is not to shrug off the hurt and damage that is done when men and women sin and especially when leaders fall in this way. At a time when our generation is in sexual overdrive it is crucial that all Christians guard their lives and that church leaders in particular address this need. Sadly in many areas of church life, there is little to separate the behaviour of believers from the world.

Many young Christians, for example, see absolutely nothing wrong with sex before marriage or with sexual experimentation. They are confused and weakened by the onslaught of worldly values. At such a time we must stand up and speak out for a return to biblical standards of behaviour once more. There is no spiritual power without moral purity.

Overcomers

Have you noticed how the language of Christians has come to differ from bible language? It is a reflection of the increasing humanistic influence on the church. The New Testament describes man's fundamental problem as sin and its remedy as salvation through Christ. But instead of speaking with this raw simplicity, the church today has adopted muddy terms and mellow tones. We hear expressions like 'coming to faith', 'getting closer to God', or 'being renewed.' But this does not help identify the real issues at stake. People need to be delivered from sin and unrighteousness by an invasion of the power of God, and to receive new birth by the Holy Spirit.

In Joseph we have a rare Old Testament example of a man overcoming sin and walking in purity. His life proved that there is no such thing as rule unless we rule sin! But as a *type* of a victorious church he also points the way to the basis of our own victory over sin.

As we've already noted Adam and Eve lost their position of dominion because of sin. Humans no longer walked in freedom and victory. But God sent his son Jesus, to reverse this situation. Dealing with sin was very much at the heart of the task of restoration. God laid an axe to the root of the problem – man's evil heart – through the personal intervention of Jesus the king.

In his death and resurrection the son of God fatally undercut Satan's kingdom and released men and women once more to be the instruments of God in the world. At the cross the allegiance between Satan and man was forever broken so we could be free to serve God. Now through Christ, God is fashioning a new race of sons in the earth. This new breed of humanity is being prepared to exercise once again the very rule and authority that Adam and Eve lost!

Joseph is also our model in this plan of restoration and rule. In him we find a man who actually made it all the way to the throne – from where he saved the world. In our introduction we noted the similarities between Joseph and Christ. We can also observe the contrasts between Joseph and Adam and see how Joseph succeeded where Adam failed:

ADAM	JOSEPH
Adam fell from a position of dominion	Joseph was raised to a position of dominion
Adam lost his destiny through rebellion	Joseph gained his destiny through submission

Adam	Joseph
Adam brought condemnation to the world	Joseph brought salvation to the world
Adam was judged	Joseph was justified

Let me make it clear that victory over sin is guaranteed to us because it has already been provided for us through the cross of Christ. Paul says we have been united with Christ in his death and resurrection (Romans 6:5). As such it is not just the penalty of sin but its very power that has been dealt with. When you are joined to Christ through new birth, you receive a transfusion of his resurrection life and nature. Hebrews 6:5 says we have, 'tasted of the powers of the age to come'.

It is that very nature alive and at work in you and me that enables us to walk free of sin. But it is only experienced through day by day surrender of your will to Christ in obedience to him. That is why in Romans 6:13-14, Paul goes on to say:

> *Do not offer the parts of your body to sin, as instruments of wickedness, but rather offer yourselves to God, as those who have been brought from death to life; and offer the parts of your body to him as instruments of righteousness. For sin shall not be your master, because you are not under law but under grace.*

Free yourself

As we have noted one of Satan's chief attacks particularly on men, is that of sexual sin. He knows that when a man compromises in this way he is severely weakened. It is one of the oldest tricks in his book. Samson, David, Solomon and many others all struggled or failed in this area of temptation. Joseph, however, overcame this enemy and stood his ground of liberty.

> *One day he went into the house to attend to his duties, and none of the household servants was inside. She caught him by his cloak and said, 'come to bed with me!' But he left the cloak in her hand and ran out of the house.*
>
> GENESIS 39:11-12

When things became too hot to handle Joseph ran from the house. This was not an act of cowardice but simply the only appropriate option he had. We must learn to run from the heat of temptation rather than try to fight it. Consider Paul's warnings, 'flee from sexual immorality' (1 Corinthians 6:18) and, 'flee the evil desires of youth', 2 Timothy 2:22.

You cannot reason with a person who is driven by passion of any kind. Joseph did the wisest thing he could; he got out of the line of fire and left the consequences to God. A spiritual battle was raging over Joseph's life. Satan was attempting to defeat him at every turn in order to frustrate God's purpose for his life. I have no doubt that Potiphar's wife was an 'enemy plant', a person demonically driven to defeat Joseph.

Is it possible to insulate our lives from defeat of this kind? Absolutely! Whatever it takes to get free and stay free, is worth it. If you are in a questionable relationship, break it off! If you have allowed yourself to become emotionally attached to someone you shouldn't, pull back now. If you need to break a habit or a fantasy, get help and do so quickly.

Free yourself, like a gazelle from the hand of the hunter,
like a bird from the snare of the fowler.

PROVERBS 6:7

Freedom must be our first and greatest priority. It is a foundation for everything else in life. It is no good asking God to do for you what you are unwilling to do yourself. You cannot make your weakness an excuse. God will rush in to help as soon as you take the first crucial step. Nothing is worth sacrificing your liberty for.

Freedom must not only be gained but also maintained by living in the fear of God. That is what lay at the heart of Joseph's own life. He feared God more than he loved sin. No doubt he felt temptation acutely. He was human just like you and me. But built into the core of his life was a love for the God who hates sin. Do all in your power to protect your life from the potential to fall and Satan will not be able to hinder your destiny.

Paying the price

When Potiphar's wife realised she couldn't get her own way, her true nature was revealed. Having been spurned by Joseph she set about to destroy him with the same passion that she had tried to bed him!

She kept his cloak beside her until his master came home. Then she told him this story: 'That Hebrew slave you brought us came to make sport of me. But as soon as I screamed for help, he left his cloak beside me and ran out of the house'.
When his master heard the story his wife told him saying, 'This is how your slave treated me', he burned with

anger. Joseph's master took him and put him in prison,
the place where the king's prisoners were confined.

Integrity will always be tested and frequently at a high personal price. Joseph suffered deeply for the stand he made and there may be negative consequences for a stand you make too. He was completely trapped and couldn't defend himself. He was a slave whereas she was the wife of a prominent citizen. Joseph was going to suffer for a crime he didn't commit while defending the man who would judge him as guilty. What an irony!

In fact, this episode foretells just another aspect of what Jesus did for us. He was innocent and yet took the punishment of the guilty. And, just like Jesus, Joseph remained silent before his accuser.

He was oppressed and afflicted, yet he did not open his
mouth. He was led like a lamb to the slaughter, and as
a sheep before his shearers is silent, so he did not open
his mouth.

ISAIAH 53:7

Just like Pilate, Potiphar condemned the innocent one, but in doing so he was unknowingly fulfilling the plan and purpose of God for the salvation of the world. Joseph had dedicated these years of his life to serving Potiphar. He had given him of his best. Now this same man was about to punish him. But Joseph did not react or retaliate.

There are times when we will suffer for our integrity as believers. It is part of our preparation for ruling with Christ. If you take a stand against sin there will be consequences. But nothing is worth the high price of excusing a moral fall.

Having dealt with the way his brothers treated him, Joseph now had to learn to forgive at an even deeper level and handle this latest injustice with grace. Just when everything in us shouts that Joseph should be rewarded for his faithfulness he is betrayed and allowed to suffer! Yet through it all he was sustained by the knowledge that God was in control of his life.

Make no mistake about it; Joseph would have been punished by Potiphar. The Egyptians were cruel to their slaves at the best of times. But to bring disgrace on your master in this way would have attracted severe punishment. He would have arrived in prison to be beaten severely: Psalm 105:16-19 says, 'They bruised his feet with shackles; his neck was put in irons'. Joseph was sent to prison to be punished for a crime he didn't commit. Injustice can sting mercilessly. Yet, just as Joseph did, we must entrust our lives to the God who justifies us.

Another eventful chapter had come to a close in Joseph's life. But God looked at his son, saw that he had passed this exam with flying colours and considered it was time to move him on in his training.

For further study

- In Potiphar's house Joseph overcame sexual temptation. Do you need to face up to any moral compromise from the past or in the present? Be very clear and specific in bringing anything to God now in confession.

- Make yourself accountable to a trusted Christian leader or friend (of the same sex) who will not be afraid to challenge you and speak truthfully to you.

- Read Romans 6 and conclude by doing what Paul says in verse 13 namely presenting the members of your body to God as instruments of righteousness.

- Now read Genesis 40 before moving on with this book.

CHAPTER 6

Prison

On the 11th February 1990 Nelson Mandela emerged from 28 years in prison to a tumultuous reception in Cape Town, South Africa. He had entered jail a criminal, the pariah of the Nationalist government. He left a hero ready to lead his country into a new era of racial justice and equality.

Mandela was initially sentenced to five years imprisonment for illegal exit from the country and incitement to strike. This was increased to life when he was subsequently found guilty of 'sabotage'. It was June 1964 when Mandela was confined on the notorious Robben Island. He was to spend the next 18 years there before transfer to a mainland prison and final release. In all it would be 21 years before he would even hold his wife's hand again.

During his captivity Mandela endured humiliation, provocation and injustice. A brilliant young lawyer, he was made to wear short trousers while breaking rocks all day in the prison yard – all the while an object of ridicule by his guards. Yet he bore it with dignity, never allowing himself to respond with self pity and always considering the suffering of his people beyond the prison walls as greater than his own.

One of the most remarkable things about Mandela at that time was that he didn't speak or behave like a victim! He came across as a man ready to take the reigns of government and lead his nation into a new era. He would eventually exchange prison for freedom and abuse for opportunity. But when he arrived on Robben Island he had no idea that three decades of captivity lay ahead. Yet he never gave up hope. He was sustained through those long years by a sense of destiny over his life.

In the same way, Joseph was now entering the darkest chapter of his life. Despite all he had gone through, his greatest challenge lay ahead. A destiny of deliverance and rule awaited, but first he must complete his preparation in this third house, the prison.

God meant it for good

A careful reading of the book of Genesis reveals that no detail of Joseph's life was left to chance. Even the circumstances of his imprisonment were carefully planned by God in advance to position him in readiness for what was to happen.

Some commentators suggest that Potiphar knew in his heart that Joseph was probably innocent. He should really have been put to death for the crime he was accused of. But not only was Joseph's life spared, Genesis 39:20 says that Potiphar put him in the royal prison-house, rather than in a jail for common criminals. By doing so he protected Joseph – and unwittingly brought into place circumstances that were to prove crucial to his future release.

But here in the dungeon, in what look like the most unfavourable of circumstances, we see the very hallmark of Joseph's journey from home to the throne. Things seemed to have gone wrong for Joseph from the moment he disclosed his dreams. But nothing could have been further from the truth. For the visible appearance always lies in complete contrast to the invisible reality of what was actually taking place. God was in control and would use everything that happened to steer him toward his destiny. Centuries later, King David interpreted his life in a remarkable way:

> *And he sent a man before them – Joseph, sold as a slave.*
> *They bruised his feet with shackles; his neck was put in*
> *irons, till what he foretold came to pass, till the word of*
> *the Lord proved him true.*
>
> PSALM 105:17-19

Notice that expression: 'the word of the Lord proved him true'. Joseph's dreams were God's word to him; a word that could not fail to come to pass. This explains why he remained free of bitterness and anger. Although imprisoned he continued to live in the assurance of God's word. God hadn't forgotten his son and Joseph trusted in this through all the painful episodes of his life.

It is impossible to understand or interpret a person's life unless you know the word of God over them. You have to get under the skin of their circumstances to appreciate this truth. Similarly your own life only makes sense when viewed in the same way. Delays, disappointments and even tragedies are not the whole story but must be seen in the light of God's word for you.

> *But Joseph said to them, 'Don't be afraid. Am I in the place of God? You intended to harm me, but God intended it for good to accomplish what is now being done, the saving of many lives'.*
>
> GENESIS 50:19-20

What an amazing confession – two statements in seeming contradiction, 'You intended to harm me, but God intended it for good'. Evil men and a good God; two opposing wills expressing themselves in the same act. Joseph understood exactly what was going on – evil could not and would not thwart God's will.

He never lost sight of the big picture and neither must you. No human being is immune from the kind of injustice and perplexity that Joseph endured. But the difference between those who overcome such things and those who are defeated by them lies in their knowledge of God's word for their lives. Don't be too hasty in passing judgment on your life until you have heard what God has to say about it.

The lowest place of all

You couldn't get lower than the prison. It was the place you were sent to be punished. It was a place where Joseph undoubtedly suffered. Later, when asking for help from the Cupbearer, he says, 'I have done nothing to deserve being put in this hole' (Genesis 40:15). Joseph was put in a hole not a hotel! He was incarcerated and left with no prospect of release. Nothing in the story suggests he would ever gain his freedom.

If you are wondering how a chapter on prison could be relevant to your life don't be tempted to skip the next few pages! Tuck these truths away in your heart for future use because you never know when you may need them. Prison is the place in your experience where you are utterly enclosed; where your circumstances have completely shut you in; where it may seem as if everything has gone wrong or your years of faithful service to God have all been in vain.

Prison is the house of disappointment, setback and loss. It is the place where you are tempted to ask, 'What were the last ten years all about?' It is the place where people watch everything they have worked for disappear. It's the house of perplexity and contradiction.

Prison is also the loneliest house. It is where you are misunderstood and the place where you are of no reputation. Oh yes, there was no lack of people in the prison with Joseph, but none of them had any real idea what he was going through on the inside. Prison is the house where people wouldn't understand even if you tried to explain!

Let's face it, good people have actually died in this house, some behind very real steel bars, others in a prison of unfulfilled promises, obscurity or deferred hope. There are many good souls like this mentioned in the book of Hebrews and they appear there because of their faith not their failure!

All these people were still living by faith when they died. They did not receive the things promised; they only saw them and welcomed them from a distance.

HEBREWS 11:13

These were all commended for their faith, yet none of them received what was promised. God had planned something better for us so that only together with us would they be made perfect.

HEBREWS 11:39-40

These who have gone before us did not die in this way because they lacked faith but because they abounded in it! For the man or woman of God there really is no other way to die apart from 'in faith'. If you don't die in faith it means you have no more dreams left, nothing more to believe God for. There is really no better way to go than 'in faith'.

So it is not necessarily wrong if a person dies with unfulfilled promises over their life – unless it's as a result of disobedience or unbelief. It shouldn't be cause for questioning their faith. It just means their vision extended beyond their lifespan. Isn't that what we should all be like?

If Joseph had died in the prison it would not have spelled his defeat. He too would have died in faith. The primary measure of faith is not the favourability of your circumstances but the strength of your heart. Right there in prison Joseph's heart was strong.

Serving in prison

At home Joseph served as a son; in Potiphar's house he served as a slave; now even while unjustly branded as a criminal, Joseph learned to serve his captors in the prison-house.

> *But while Joseph was there in the prison, the Lord was with him; he showed him kindness and granted him favour in the eyes of the prison warden. So the warden put Joseph in charge of all those held in the prison and he was made responsible for all that was done there. The warden paid no attention to anything under Joseph's care, because the Lord was with Joseph and gave him success in whatever he did.*
>
> GENESIS 39:20-21.

Once again the testimony of Genesis is that 'God was with Joseph'. What was notable during Joseph's stay in Potiphar's house is repeated in the prison. Why? Because nothing had changed inside Joseph's heart. He walked in forgiveness toward those who sinned against him. He trusted God with his life. He gave himself as a servant to those around him. He was the same man.

When Genesis says the Lord showed Joseph kindness and granted him favour, the word 'kindness' is the Hebrew word *chesed,* one of the most precious words in the bible. It signifies God's covenant love, faithfulness and mercy. The word 'favour' is the Hebrew word *chen,* meaning an expression of God's grace.

These two frequently paired bible words are central to describing God's covenant nature. Joseph may have been in prison but he was not under the jurisdiction of the prison. He was overshadowed by the covenant love, protection and favour of Jehovah. Prison did not have the power to separate him from God's divine covenant love. God did not send him to this house to be punished but to be prepared.

Even in incarceration Joseph served his captors with the same spirit of excellence and integrity that marked his earlier life. The hand of God was upon him and this was recognised by the prison warden who promoted Joseph in his responsibilities. As far as Joseph was concerned the prison was no more than the environment in which God had placed him at that time. Prison didn't prevent him from serving or prospering. Neither did it hinder the grace of God upon him. He may have been in a prison but the prison did not control him!

All of us must learn how to serve in the prison experiences of life. However difficult, they are simply the setting where God has chosen for us to serve at that time. Every position the person of faith finds themselves is the house of God's choice for that moment. As such you can serve and succeed wherever you are, however unlikely the location.

When you feel crushed by rejection, the best thing you can do is serve God. When you feel upset by injustice, the most powerful thing you can do is serve God. Satan may tempt you to indulge in self-pity, but you must do the opposite and occupy yourself with serving the Lord. By doing this you will defeat the spirit of self-pity outright.

Supernatural serving

> *Some time later, the cupbearer and the baker of the king of Egypt offended their master, the king of Egypt. Pharaoh was angry with his two officials, the chief cupbearer and the chief baker, and put them in custody in the house of the captain of the guard, in the same prison where Joseph was confined. The captain of the guard assigned them to Joseph and he attended them.*
>
> GENESIS 40:1-4

One day the dull routine of prison life was interrupted by the arrival of two new prisoners. Pharaoh's cupbearer and baker had both fallen out of favour with their master. We are not told anything of their crime, but it was evidently serious. Again, we see the hand of God at work in perfectly positioning Joseph for his divine purpose. Not only were these two men thrown into the same dungeon, but as Joseph served them over the course of time a friendship grew between them.

After some time in captivity, we learn that they both had dreams on the same night.

When Joseph came to them the next morning, he saw
that they were dejected. So he asked Pharaoh's officials
who were in custody with him in his master's house,
'Why are your faces so sad today?' 'We both had dreams',
they answered, 'but there is no one to interpret them'.
Then Joseph said to them, 'Do not interpretations belong
to God? Tell me your dreams'.

Genesis 40:6-8

Joseph was blessed with the gifts of dreams and the interpretation
of dreams. In prison he not only served practically, but welcomed
the opportunity to serve with these anointed supernatural gifts.
He had no idea of the outcome when he committed himself to
help these men.

So the chief cupbearer told Joseph his dream. He said to
him, 'In my dream I saw a vine in front of me, and on
the vine were three branches. As soon as it budded, it
blossomed and its clusters ripened into grapes. Pharaoh's
cup was in my hand, and I took the grapes, squeezed
them into Pharaoh's cup and put the cup in his hand.'
    'This is what it means', Joseph said to him.
'The three branches are three days. Within three days
Pharaoh will lift up your head and restore you to your
position and you will put Pharaoh's cup in his hand,
just as you used to do when you were his cupbearer. But
when all goes well with you, remember me and show me
kindness; mention me to Pharaoh and get me out of this
prison. For I was forcibly carried off from the land of the
Hebrews, and even here I have done nothing to deserve
being put in a dungeon'.

Genesis 40:9-14

The moment he became aware of the interpretation of the cupbearer's dream Joseph faced a choice. Should he assist a man who would soon be released from the prison? The flesh would say, 'why should I do anything for this man when I have no prospect of release?' But Joseph was genuinely pleased that the cupbearer would get promoted ahead of him. Through this incident we gain another insight into his remarkable character; he was willing to help another man get on regardless of his own interests.

You are only ready for rule when you can promote others before yourself. This is the mark of true freedom. Only a free person can leave their own life in God's hands and serve the welfare of someone else. There was nothing perverse about this. Joseph was not acting like a martyr or behaving like a doormat for someone to walk all over. He simply delighted in adding value to the lives of others.

One further point is worth observing; Joseph had every reason to be cautious around the business of dream interpretation. Don't forget his first adventure in this witnessed the start of all his troubles! Why put his head in the noose again? Why take any more chances? But he was ready to have another go! He refused to bury his gift – what an example for you and I. Don't let a bad experience from the past prevent you from believing God and stepping out again.

> *When the chief baker saw that Joseph had given a favourable interpretation, he said to Joseph, 'I too had a dream: On my head were three baskets of bread. In the top basket were all kinds of baked goods for Pharaoh, but the birds were eating them out of the basket on my head'.*

*'This is what it means', Joseph said. 'The three
baskets are three days. Within three days Pharaoh will
lift off your head and hang you on a tree. And the birds
will eat away your flesh'.*

Genesis 40:16-19

What a dilemma Joseph faced with the baker's dream! What
might be the backlash of bearing bad news? Why risk the
consequence? Why bring trouble on himself? Wouldn't it
be better to feign complete ignorance? But Joseph behaved
consistently toward each man. He acted without regard to the
personal consequences and left his case with God. For Joseph
the issue was not whether he could always be positive and
encouraging, but whether could tell the truth.

There is a profound lesson for us here. You are not ready
for rule unless you can be truthful with people! Many occasions
arise in leadership and responsibility when you are faced with
the disagreeable task of straight talking. Confrontation is never
a pleasure but sometimes it is unavoidable. You must overcome
the fear of man rather than evade the opportunity of helping
someone face the truth honestly; as Proverbs 27:5 says, 'Better
is open rebuke than hidden love'.

Open rebuke is better than hidden love because hidden
love is not actually real love at all! If your relationship cannot
sustain some simple honesty you need to question what kind of
relationship it really is!

As they took their leave of Joseph, he had just one request
of the cup bearer:

*'When all goes well with you, remember me and show
me kindness; mention me to Pharaoh and get me out of
this prison. For I was forcibly carried off from the land*

> *of the Hebrews, and even here I have done nothing to*
> *deserve being put in a dungeon.'*
>
> GENESIS 40:14-15

Joseph was not selfish in asking for help. Neither did his request signify a lack of trust in God. Although he served in every situation of life, he was no-one's dogs-body! He was not a Uriah Heap character. If there was a legitimate way of rectifying the injustice done to him then he would take it. Joseph knew the difference between right and wrong.

But now all he could do was to wait for the cupbearer to deliver on his promise. Into the bleakness of the prison, a ray of hope had come. Joseph had been through so much and had waited so patiently. Now an answer was tantalisingly close. Surely his moment of release was approaching?

Can you imagine the temptations Joseph faced when he realised the cupbearer had forgotten to help him? Days turned to weeks and weeks to months. A full two years passed and still he heard nothing. It was now that he faced his darkest hour and his most severe test. There was now literally no human hope of ever being released!

As we approach this moment in Joseph's life we should be aware that we are treading on holy ground. Beneath the bible's brief description of events, powerful forces were at work. A cosmic drama was being played out within the walls of the prison and we are going to unpack that drama now.

For Further Study

- Are you facing any kind of prison experience right now? Are you battling with discouragement and perplexity or do you even feel like giving up? Be honest and identify what the actual source of this is. Ask God to speak to you as you continue to read this book.

- In what ways can you serve others in your present circumstances; firstly with your natural abilities and secondly with supernatural gifts?

- Think of someone you can promote ahead of yourself and begin praying for their success.

- Now read Genesis 41.

CHAPTER 7

Satan Defeated

There is a powerful spiritual element to the story of Joseph. Satan was monitoring the events of his life closely and maintained a special interest in destroying him. The devil was aware that God had chosen Joseph for a mission to save the world. He had tried, through temptations and trials, to conquer him without success. But here at last was an irresistible opportunity for attack, an internal battle with self pity and despair of the most intense kind. Satan threw his full wrath at Joseph in order to defeat him.

This servant of God was now utterly and completely tested. When he realised that he had been forgotten by the cupbearer, the last flicker of human hope was extinguished. Joseph had done all he could with the best motive and it had achieved nothing. He had served freely and overcome every temptation, for what end? There was every reason for him to think he would die behind bars.

In a prison house experience like this you have to overcome the deepest temptation to self-pity, dashed hopes, perplexity and despair. Perplexity is where you can find no answer for what is happening. Despair is when you have no more internal resources left to draw on and you want to give up. Joseph faced all of these things!

I am sure that Jesus too was tempted to give up at times. We saw earlier, from Hebrews 4:15, that he was tempted in every way just like us ... yet without sinning. It was necessary for him to taste every temptation common to man in order to fulfil his God-given destiny.

So too for us, facing the temptation to quit may not just be a possibility but a necessity on our journey. Don't let it become a cause of alarm; it's a valley to be passed through in preparation for the throne. Why? Because when you feel like giving up you know that your own strength has come to an end. Whatever is left after you have faced the temptation to quit is due to the power of God. You can only come through it by divine strength – and that is exactly what God wants.

If you are going through a prison house experience just now, take courage and wait for the Lord. He is the God of resurrection. He knows how to raise his people up!

The cosmic drama

Satan thought he finally had Joseph in his jaws. Surely no human being could endure such extreme testing and still trust in God? So the devil went in for the kill. He ground Joseph's soul like powder. He assaulted and molested his mind. He crushed him like corn beneath a millstone. He did everything to provoke him to rise up against God; to accuse him of injustice, to indulge in self-justification and self-pity.

All that remained in Joseph was his trust in the promises of God. This was the only weapon left in his armoury. He had no human hope, no reputation, no possessions, and no friends in high places. But what looked like the end of the road for Joseph was no dead end; it was about to be his place of triumph, his finest hour. Consider again, what David prophesied about this experience of Joseph:

> *They bruised his feet with shackles; his neck was put in irons, till what he foretold came to pass, till the word of the Lord proved him true.*
>
> PSALM 105:18-19

I am convinced that Joseph did not yield to the temptation to doubt God's word. To do so would have spelt his defeat. Furthermore he had no reason to doubt. The integrity of God's word alone was sufficient ground for his victory over despair or self-pity. Joseph's dream remained alive. He did more than cling to it in desperation. He rested in it because its author is *El-Shaddai*, the 'all sufficient one', the highest authority on earth and the God who would vindicate him.

There was nothing left to try in Joseph's heart. He didn't allow his spirit to be defiled with anger or self-justification. He trusted in God despite his sufferings and refused to blame God for anything. At last Satan fell back defeated. There was nothing more he could do. A man in submission to God had overcome the devil.

Satan should have learned his lesson through what happened with Joseph, because in the course of time another man, Jesus of Nazareth, would arise, sent by God in exactly the same way for the salvation of the world.

Just like Joseph, Jesus would be tested at every point. Satan would throw every possible temptation and accusation at him. Just like Joseph, Jesus would be tempted to give up, to justify himself, to yield to the most intense feelings of rejection and self pity. But history would repeat itself.

Satan should have learned from his experience at the hands of Joseph – you cannot defeat a man or woman living in total submission to the will of God

Jesus defeated Satan in the prison house of Calvary just as Joseph defeated Satan in an Egyptian jail. The defeat he suffered at Joseph's hands was destined to be repeated on a far grander scale in Christ.

But there's a yet deeper mystery at work in the story: for Satan was not the master of the situation, just the unwitting tool of God in the preparation of his servant Joseph. Satan was actually serving God's purpose without realising it. The devil is God's devil. When we are inside God's will, Satan is God's instrument for our glory. When we are outside of God's will Satan is a fearsome foe. He can only harm those living independently of the will of God.

This is an awesome truth that is only understood by living in submission; if you resort to anger, revenge, self pity or unbelief you will be swallowed up by those demons. Place your whole life at God's disposal however, and you'll find that even those things that were meant to harm you will actually work for your good.

In truth, Joseph was being prepared by God in secret, away from the public gaze. God was crafting his life in preparation for the throne. Listen to these words of Charles Swindoll:

*All whom God uses greatly are first hidden in the secret
of his presence, away from the pride of man. It is there
our vision clears. It is there the silt drops from the current
of our life and our faith begins to grasp His arm.*

CHARLES SWINDOLL,
JOSEPH, A MAN OF INTEGRITY AND FORGIVENESS

Just like Joseph, Jesus overcame Satan and God exalted him to
the throne. Today there is a man on the throne of heaven who
has secured the salvation of the earth. Jesus sits at God's right
hand from where he has opened the scroll, the title deed of the
earth. He is feeding the nations with the life-giving manna of
his word. He is pouring out his Holy Spirit to deliver men and
women from oppression and sickness. He is gathering his end-
time church and, finally, he will reconcile the Jewish people to
himself before his return in triumph!

The enemy unmasked

We should not be too dogmatic about the origins of Satan but
it would seem from certain key scriptures that he was a high
ranking angel, endowed with particular beauty and trusted with
special responsibilities. Among these was the custodianship of
the earth. The prophet Ezekiel describes it this way:

*You were the model of perfection, full of wisdom and
perfect in beauty. You were in Eden the garden of God;
every precious stone adorned you; ruby, topaz and
emerald, chrysolite, onyx and jasper, sapphire, turquoise
and beryl. Your settings and mountings were made of
gold; on the day you were created they were prepared. You
were anointed as a guardian cherub, for so I ordained*

you. You were on the holy mount of God; you walked among the fiery stones.

EZEKIEL 28:12-14

At some point pride entered his heart: 'You were blameless in your ways from the day you were created till wickedness was found in you', Ezekiel goes on to say (Ezekiel 28:14-15). Satan was jealous of the worship due to God alone and as a result he was expelled from heaven.

How you have fallen from heaven, O morning star, son of the dawn! You have been cast down to the earth, you who once laid low the nations! You said in your heart, 'I will ascend to heaven; I will raise my throne above the stars of God; I will sit enthroned on the mount of assembly, on the uttermost heights of the sacred mountain. I will ascend above the tops of the clouds; I will make myself like the Most High'. But you are brought down to the grave, to the depths of the pit.

ISAIAH 14:12-15

It is all too easy to take a simplistic view of the devil; to see him as the originator of unfettered evil, a law unto himself whose activities lie completely outside the will of God. But to think this way would be a big mistake. God is sovereign over all creation, the good the bad and the ugly. Everyone and everything, even Satan, serves a purpose! The fact that God has not yet destroyed him demonstrates in itself that he is still of use in God's will.

Satan has been active throughout human history and, as we see, the life of Joseph was no exception. Joseph was able to overcome Satan's schemes because of his absolute submission to the will of God. He understood the truth that God rules over all the affairs of man. It lies at the heart of his cry to his brothers, 'You intended it for evil, but God meant it for good'.

This is a profound mystery but one that we must grasp in order to interpret our own lives correctly. When we live in submission to the will of God, Satan has to serve it too, because he is powerless in the face of such obedience.

Satan's character

The parallel stories of Joseph and Christ offer a fascinating insight into the character of the devil. Satan has a personality. He is driven by pride and pride is the greatest form of moral blindness. The reason he keeps suffering the same defeat boils down to this very issue. Satan is the most arrogant creature in the universe. He is clever and crafty, but his pride will not allow him to think objectively. He cannot behave any differently than his nature will allow.

History provides us with some interesting examples of satanic character. This character is repeatedly superimposed on human personalities. We see evidence of this in the lives of Nebuchadnezzar, the Emperor Nero, Stalin and Hitler to name but a few. Haman, in the book of Esther, is perhaps the most striking biblical comparison to Satan we can find; this man was driven by a devilish obsession to destroy the Jewish people. His hatred was inflamed by a personal grudge against a man called Mordecai and all because this godly Jew would not bow before him.

A high-ranking government official or Vizier, Haman used his access to King Xerxes to persuade him to pass a law that would spell the extermination of the Jews. This fact alone demonstrates the way in which he was being manipulated by the devil. Satan was constantly seeking an opportunity to wipe out the Jewish people, because from them would eventually be born the Messiah of all mankind, Jesus.

This dastardly plot to kill the Jews was discovered by Mordecai who alerted his niece Queen Esther. Esther knew that in order to save her people she would have to expose Haman's wicked scheme. Acting shrewdly and wisely to see this evil enemy dealt with, she used his own pride as bait to trap him.

Esther took her courage in both hands and requested an audience before the King. When he extended the golden sceptre of his favour towards her, her simple request was to invite him to a banquet in his honour and to bring along Haman. She was setting a trap to which Haman was oblivious. Arrogance prevented him from seeing through this 'long con', this divine hustle. Meanwhile this violent man carried on with his wicked designs, by arranging for a custom-built gallows to be erected – a gallows for Mordecai.

On the second day of the banquet, Esther sprang her trap on the unsuspecting plotter. She interceded before the King for her people against him. The king pronounced judgment against Haman and he was hanged on the self-same gallows he had built for Mordecai.

Haman was defeated not by force but by the wisdom of Esther – in the same way that Jesus defeated Satan, not by force but by the wisdom of God. Esther used Haman's own pride to lure him to the place of his own defeat and he was conquered by his own diabolical plans. In exactly the same way, Satan thought he would defeat Jesus at the cross. His own pride blinded him and that self-same cross proved to be the place of his own downfall.

Satan's pride blinded him to God's wisdom for his defeat

With Haman overcome, Esther continued with wisdom and courage, persuading the king to issue a decree that enabled the Jews to defend themselves against attack. Using her unhindered access to the throne she became an instrument of salvation on a massive scale.

The triumph of submission

What parallel do we find with Christ? When the Saviour dropped his guard in the garden of Gethsemane, Satan couldn't resist the opportunity to move in for the kill. He had sought to trap Jesus on many occasions, but hadn't been able to because his time had not yet come. Now for some reason that the devil just didn't understand Jesus was volunteering his enemy access. In Luke 22:53 Jesus says, 'This is your hour when darkness reigns'. Now Satan thought he could do what he wanted with the son of God. His pride simply wouldn't permit him to ask why Jesus should make himself defenceless.

It was an opportunity too good to miss, of which Satan took full advantage. He engineered and manipulated the events of the trial, of Jesus' suffering and the guilty verdict. He hounded Christ all the way to the cross, yet unbeknown to him God never relinquished control. This was actually a sting operation of cosmic proportions.

On one occasion Jesus said:

The reason my Father loves me is that I lay down my life – only to take it up again. No one takes it from me, but I lay it down of my own accord.

JOHN 10:17-18

But the only reason Satan was able to act against Jesus was because Christ allowed him to. There at Calvary he was able to have his way with the Son of God *by consent*. Just as with Joseph, Satan assaulted and tormented him, knowing that should Jesus rise up in self justification for even a second, he would have won.

But Jesus defeated Satan through his submission to his Father. Finally, when Satan could do no more, Jesus pronounced, 'it is finished'. He yielded up his spirit to his father and salvation's plan was accomplished.

As a victorious man, Christ descended into Hades, the place of the dead, there to claim its keys and the keys of death. Then on the third day, his swift promotion to the throne of the universe began! From death to life he came and appeared over forty days to his disciples. Finally, from the earth and through the heavens he passed in a glorious victory procession until he appeared once more before the throne of God, from which he had been sent.

Let's return to Joseph; it was there in that dark and awful prison that he overcame Satan and won the right to the throne that God had prepared for him all along. Faith in a dream alone could not do it. He had to overcome the enemy of his soul and that is what he did with such distinction.

Divine appointment

When two full years had passed, Pharaoh had a dream: He was standing by the Nile, when out of the river there came up seven cows, sleek and fat, and they grazed among the reeds. After them, seven other cows, ugly and gaunt, came up out of the Nile and stood beside those on the riverbank. And the cows that were ugly and gaunt ate up the seven sleek, fat cows. Then Pharaoh woke up.

He fell asleep again and had a second dream:
Seven heads of grain, healthy and good, were growing
on a single stalk. After them, seven other heads of grain
sprouted – thin and scorched by the east wind. The thin
heads of grain swallowed up the seven healthy heads.
Then Pharaoh woke up; it had been a dream.

GENESIS 41:1-17

When the season was up God put a dream in the mind of Pharaoh. He woke startled and disturbed. This was no ordinary dream and he puzzled deeply over it. He went back to sleep and dreamt a second time in similar vein. Pharaoh instinctively knew these dreams were supernatural in origin and must be interpreted.

He called for his astrologers and magicians but no one could help the king with the meaning of his dreams. At this moment the cupbearer remembered Joseph and reported his own experience to Pharaoh. Joseph was immediately summoned to appear before the king.

So Pharaoh sent for Joseph, and he was quickly brought
from the dungeon. When he had shaved and changed his
clothes, he came before Pharaoh.

GENESIS 41:14

This particular day began like any other for Joseph; the same oppressive surroundings, the same monotonous routine. Suddenly, palace guards arrived and summoned him with haste to appear before Pharaoh. Joseph knew nothing of what had happened the previous night. He had no idea why he was being called to the King. But when he did appear in the palace he was composed and confident. How could he behave like this after being locked up for so long? The reason was simple. He was living in readiness for this moment!

For Joseph there was actually very little difference between the prison and the palace. The distance between the third and fourth house was the smallest of all. Although such places might seem light-years apart, for Joseph there was just one step. He was already thinking like a prince in his heart and living like a prince in the prison. He may have worn jail clothes, but he walked around his cell like a free man.

When the moment arrived he stepped confidently into Pharaoh's presence. The only thing he had to clean up was his outward appearance. Joseph had a shave and a change of clothes. He didn't need to sort his attitudes out. No extra time was requested in order to seek the forgiveness of anyone. He didn't need to repent of anger or self-pity. He was living with a clear conscience and a ready heart.

No character change occurred between Joseph's last day in prison and his first day in the palace!

Readiness cannot wait. No matter what your circumstances you must live in a state of preparedness before God. The days of getting ready are over. We must be prepared for our appointment with destiny when it arrives for it is a moment that knocks without warning.

When Joseph appeared before Pharaoh he had no idea whether this was going to be the real thing or another false dawn. Yet once again he served another man regardless of himself. He used his supernatural gift to interpret Pharaoh's dreams. He pushed the door and left God to open it. At that moment Joseph's future hung in the balance. His destiny rested on a knife edge. He could have been set free or sent back to prison.

Pharaoh said to Joseph, 'I had a dream, and no one is able to interpret it. But I have heard it said of you that when you hear a dream you can interpret it'.

'I cannot do it'; Joseph replied to Pharaoh, 'But God will give Pharaoh the answer he desires'.

GENESIS 41:14-16

Joseph nailed his colours to the mast immediately. His faith was no private matter. If this was a divine appointment it could carry the weight of giving God the credit. Joseph was in no mind to compromise at this stage of the game. Pharaoh's heart had been prepared by God for this moment and he was open. He related the sequence of dreams and Joseph immediately gives the interpretation.

'The seven good cows are seven years, and the seven good heads of grain are seven years; it is one and the same dream. The seven lean, ugly cows that came up afterward are seven years, and so are the seven worthless heads of grain scorched by the east wind: they are seven years of famine.'

GENESIS 41:26-27

Joseph spelled it out to Egypt's ruler: the land would experience a seven year abundance followed by a seven year famine like no other they had ever known for its severity. It would wipe away even the memory of the good years!

"And now let Pharaoh look for a discerning and wise man and put him in charge of the land of Egypt. Let Pharaoh appoint commissioners over the land to take a fifth of the harvest of Egypt during the seven years of abundance. They should collect all the food of these good

*years that are coming and store up the grain under the
authority of Pharaoh, to be kept in the cities for food.
This food should be held in reserve for the country, to
be used during the seven years of famine that will come
upon Egypt so that the country will not be ruined by
the famine.'*

GENESIS 41:33-36

Not only did Joseph offer divine knowledge, he volunteered
divine wisdom for Pharaoh too. He proposed a strategy for
national rescue that Pharaoh accepted:

*The plan seemed good to Pharaoh and his officials. So
Pharaoh asked them, 'Can we find anyone like this man,
one in whom is the Spirit of God?'*

*Then Pharaoh said to Joseph, 'Since God has made
all this known to you, there is no one so discerning and
wise as you. You shall be in charge of my palace, and
all my people are to submit to your orders. Only with
respect to the throne will I be greater than you'.*

GENESIS 41:37-40

Pharaoh's heart had been prepared by God and he accepted
both the solution and the man who proposed it. The amazing
thing about the repositioning of Joseph's life is that he neither
grasped nor refused it. He simply embraced this extraordinary
opportunity as the will of God. It was an act of divine resurrection.
Joseph was being raised up, just like Jesus, from the dead, to rule
the world as a servant of its salvation. But having been raised
up by God, Joseph accepted the opportunity without apology or
reluctance. He stood there as a proven man – someone in whom
there was neither intimidation nor ambition.

God has the same purpose for you and me as part of his overcoming church of the end time. God's people are not destined for obscurity but for authority. But the church that reigns only does so in resurrection power. There is no other kind of authority.

Joseph didn't see this as a moment to get even. He didn't call for the cupbearer, mention Potiphar or his wife or seek to promote his own cause. He had died in prison! His only thought was to help Pharaoh and the Egyptian people. A reigning church is taken up with the cause of Christ to save a dying world. Exactly how it does this is modelled for us through the account of Joseph's new life in the palace.

For Further Study

- Jesus overcame Satan through submission to his Father. Make a deliberate choice to submit every attitude and emotion of yours to God right now. Bring everything under his rule, proclaiming yourself dead to it all.

- Preparation was a key issue in Joseph's life. Are there character areas that need to change for you to be ready for God to move you to the next house? If so, face them with God and embrace the necessary change.

- Are you able to speak out to those in positions of influence without compromise? Deal with anything that may hinder such readiness.

CHAPTER 8

The Palace

We all love stories of redemption – the innocent victim coming back against overwhelming odds, restored and vindicated. One of the most popular recent tales of this kind is portrayed in the film *The Shawshank Redemption*. It tells the story of Andy Defrane, a young lawyer falsely convicted of the murder of his wife. He is given a life sentence which he must serve at a brutal prison. It is the 1950s in one of the USA's southern states and the jail is ruled over by a tyrannical warden.

Through patience, strength of character and sheer brilliance, Andy Defrane eventually manages to escape. You can't help feeling a surge of elation as he finally emerges from a sewer pipe beyond the prison fence and you know he is really free. Left behind is the warden who has taken his own life and corrupt guards now under arrest.

I have noticed that such stories of redemption fall into two broad categories; they end in either reconciliation or revenge! *The Shawshank Redemption* falls squarely into the second category along with a host of others from *The Count of Monte Cristo* all the way to *Rambo!* Joseph's story, however, definitely falls into the first category. It is a chronicle of forgiveness and reconciliation.

This virtuous man not only had the right, but also the opportunity to make sure all who had treated him so badly received their just desserts! But that's not how this particular account of redemption went; it does not end in a blood-fest of retribution. Instead, it leads to the restoration of broken relationships and the salvation of a hungry world. This was only possible because Joseph submitted to God in his suffering rather than allowing vengeance to fill his heart.

As we have seen already, it is a story paralleled in the life of Jesus.

> *During the days of Jesus' life on earth, he offered up prayers and petitions with loud cries and tears to the one who was able to save him from death, and he was heard because of his reverent submission. Although he was a son, he learned obedience from what he suffered and, once made perfect, he became the source of eternal salvation for all who obey him and was designated by God to be high priest in the order of Melchizedek.*
>
> HEBREWS 5:7-9

In describing his journey to the cross, the book of Hebrews says that Jesus learned obedience not bitterness through what he suffered. The reason he didn't seek revenge for what he suffered was the same as Joseph's; he submitted his life to God in his suffering. He may have been the favoured son of God, but he did not escape an experience of suffering that prepared him for his ministry of salvation. We too face the same choice in our experience of life.

Now if we are children, then we are heirs – heirs of God and co-heirs with Christ, if indeed we share in his sufferings in order that we may also share in his glory.

ROMANS 8:17

Suffering isn't exactly what most of us have at the top of our wish-list! But to reign with Christ we must first also suffer with him. To experience the power of his resurrection we must first embrace the death of self. The level of authority God wants his people to possess demands a complete work of the cross in our lives. There can be no room for selfish ambition, power seeking or self-serving.

We learn obedience the same way as Joseph and Jesus, through suffering. Suffering is a necessary qualification for the exercise of authority that comes from the throne. People who occupy the palace are dead men made alive; they are the only kind suited for the task.

Thirteen years had passed since Joseph entered Egypt bound as a captive. He had endured betrayal, slavery, injustice, prison, crushed hopes and abandonment. Now his suffering was complete and he was free. He could walk in the palace gardens, feast on the finest food of his choice and talk to whomever he pleased.

And yet he was not entirely free. He may have been out of the prison but he was still walking a pathway of destiny. No longer behind bars, Joseph was still a prisoner to the will of God and he was not about to retire into obscurity.

The palace he entered as a prisoner was about to become his final home in God's purpose for his life. In prison Joseph had suffered; now in the palace he was ready to serve.

Jesus is Lord!

We have already seen how the story of Joseph mirrors that of Jesus. He was rejected by his own people, betrayed and sentenced to death as a guilty man. And we have seen that just like Joseph, Jesus overcame every attack Satan threw against him. At the cross he defeated Satan and God raised him up to the highest place from where he is implementing a world-wide plan of salvation.

Joseph's promotion from prison to the palace is a picture of Jesus' resurrection and ascension to the courts of heaven and the description in Genesis 41 gives us some amazing insights into this advancement.

Exalted and honoured

> *Then Pharaoh took his signet ring from his finger and put it on Joseph's finger. He dressed him in robes of fine linen and put a gold chain around his neck. He had him ride in a chariot as his second in command, and men shouted before him, 'Make way!' Thus he put him in charge of the whole land of Egypt.*
>
> GENESIS 41:42-43

The signet ring denoted authority. It was how the King 'rubber stamped' his wishes. It meant Joseph carried the same authority as Pharaoh. The fine clothes and gold chain were signs of distinction. Then Pharaoh had Joseph honoured in a royal procession at which men honoured him before the people as he appeared.

It was the same for Jesus in his ascension. When he returned to the presence of his father, God glorified his son before all the heavenly beings. Psalm 24 foretells this amazing event:

Lift up your heads, Oh you gates; that the king of glory
may come in. Who is he, this king of glory? The Lord
Almighty – he is the king of glory.

PSALM 24:9-10

Seated at the right hand of the throne

'You shall be in charge of my palace, and all my people
are to submit to your orders. Only with respect to the
throne will I be greater than you.'

GENESIS 41:40

Joseph was raised up to the highest place in the kingdom; only
Pharaoh was greater. So too, after Jesus rose from the dead and
ascended to heaven, God the father seated him at his own right
hand in glory. Peter said that Jesus had been, 'exalted to the right
hand of God', (Acts 2:32). Jesus has been given the highest place
heaven can afford.

Invested with all authority

Then Pharaoh said to Joseph, 'I am Pharaoh, but without
your word no one will lift hand or foot in all Egypt'.

GENESIS 41:44

Pharaoh invested authority into Joseph's words. Joseph could
now speak with his name and his word would be done. In an
even more glorious way, God the father has invested authority
to his son, 'Then Jesus came to them and said, "All authority in
heaven and earth has been given to me"', (Matthew 28:18).

Philippians 2:10 says that, 'at the name of Jesus every knee
shall bow', and Peter said that he must reign until every enemy

becomes his footstool (Acts 2:35). The name of Jesus carries all authority in heaven and earth!

Saviour of the world

Genesis 41:45 says that Pharaoh gave Joseph the name *Zaphenath-Paneah*. Literally translated this means 'saviour of the world'. Pharaoh recognised that the salvation of the world was in the hands of Joseph. So too, God the father has given to his son, 'the name above every name', (Philippians 2:9). The name Jesus means 'God is saviour'. Jesus is the only one appointed by God to save the world from its sins and in Acts 4:12 Peter declared that salvation is found in no other name.

The world comes to Christ

> *The seven years of abundance in Egypt came to an end, and the seven years of famine began, just as Joseph had said. There was famine in all the other lands, but in the whole land of Egypt there was food.*
>
> GENESIS 42:53-54

There was now food for the hungry because God had his man on the throne at last! It's impossible to separate these two principles of sovereignty and salvation. Because Jesus occupies the throne he is able to save those who come to him. Only in this way will mankind's emptiness be satisfied.

Outside of Christ, men and women are dying from spiritual and moral famine. Nothing in the world will ever satisfy and the best it can offer will ultimately fail. Conversely, everything mankind needs is found in Christ. There is more than enough in him to satisfy every man and woman.

When all Egypt began to feel the famine, the people cried to Pharaoh for food. Then Pharaoh told all the Egyptians, 'Go to Joseph and do what he tells you'.

GENESIS 41:55

People do not come to Christ simply because they have a need but when they *feel* their need. It wasn't until they were hungry that the people began to turn to Pharaoh, and through him, to Joseph for help. So too, men and women turn to God when all their other options have failed. When they feel the famine they make their move. I have never seen a person get saved who did not first experience an acute need. It is this need that breaks down stubborn pride and intellectual resistance.

Members of my own family have come to Christ this same way. My father for instance, was a self-made, self-sufficient man until that is, the doctors could do nothing about his cancer. Then he turned to God!

When the people appeared at Pharaoh's doorstep, he pointed them to Joseph. In the same way, God the father points the world to his son for salvation. Pharaoh says, 'Go to Joseph'. God says, 'Go to Jesus'. Jesus is the man God raised up to be the source of world salvation. It is not found in religion, self-help or even Christian devotions. You can't get the goods without going through Jesus!

In reading this book you may have realised that you do not know Christ as your personal saviour and Lord. You can change that today. At the end of this chapter is a prayer of commitment. Use it to ask Jesus into your life to give you a fresh start as a new-born Christian.

When the famine had spread all over the whole country, Joseph opened the storehouses and sold grain to the Egyptians, for the famine was severe throughout Egypt. And all the countries came to Egypt to buy grain from Joseph, because the famine was severe in the entire world.

GENESIS 41:56-57

What began as a trickle turned into a flood. First just Egypt was rescued; then as news spread the whole world turned its attention to Egypt and its governor. But God has always had the whole world in view. Salvation will not be confined to certain corners of the globe. Revival cannot be limited to particular countries or cultures. Even the millions who still remain trapped in the darkness of false religions and ideologies will turn to the living God. The father will bring the world to his son. This is his promise to Jesus, 'Ask of me and I will make the nations your inheritance', Psalm 2:8.

The God who exalts

What do we make of this fourth house for Joseph? What is the significance for us, of his years in the palace? Remember, all his life had been a preparation for this. God had been moulding him for this moment. Life in the palace would be marked by power and prestige, freedom and fulfilment, but it would also present some of Joseph's greatest challenges.

What we find in the fourth house is Joseph exercising tremendous authority from the throne of Egypt with a pure and proven heart. It demonstrates how God's people, risen with Christ, can actually behave. Joseph was entrusted with unimaginable power, yet not once did he use it for his own ends. He was a truly meek man. Meekness is humility in power. It isn't weakness; it is a proven person exercising great authority.

Jesus said, 'Blessed are the meek for they shall inherit the earth', Matthew 5:5.

Likewise, God is determined to raise up a church to which he can entrust such authority. The world will not be saved by a rag-tag band of carnal Christians but an army of heavenly saints walking in the authority and anointing of their God. We dare not run from our appointment in the palace! These closing chapters of Genesis show us what such an army looks like.

Joseph shows us how a heavenly, palace-people behave when they occupy the throne

Joseph enjoyed privilege and prestige beyond description – without it tainting his heart. He administrated an international famine relief strategy. He handled the reconciliation of his brothers. Finally he arranged the reception of his family in Egypt. Joseph's life in the palace is a model of God's people ruling and reigning with Christ from the heavenly places.

The first challenge for Joseph in his new situation was the sheer extravagance of his new life. The contrast between prison and palace couldn't have been more extreme. Having seen how he maintained his integrity in the privations of the prison, God was pleased to shower untold blessing on his son Joseph. As lord of Egypt, he would have enjoyed the most opulent of lifestyles.

Let's be clear though, Joseph never sought prosperity for its own sake. It followed him simply as a result of an obedient life. But neither did he refuse this newfound privilege. It takes grace to be abased. It also requires grace to abound and be exalted. Joseph was content in either.

Biblical prosperity is not measured by material affluence but by the development of your faith. Yet God does call some people to the stewardship of great wealth and we should rejoice when it is handled with wisdom and humility as it was with Joseph.

The two sons

Soon after arriving in the Palace, Pharaoh gave Joseph a wife, Asenath daughter of an Egyptian priest, and they had two sons. The naming of children carried great significance and those Joseph gave his sons show us what was going on in his heart at this time of transition in his life:

> *Before the years of famine came, two sons were born to Joseph by Asenath daughter of Potiphera priest of On. Joseph named his firstborn Manasseh and said, 'It is because God has made me forget all my trouble and all my father's household'. The second son he named Ephraim and said, 'It is because God has made me fruitful in the land of my suffering'.*
>
> GENESIS 41:50-52

The first boy's name Manasseh comes from the Hebrew word *nashah*, meaning to forget. God had removed the painful sting of the memory of all he had endured. We know it was not the memory itself that was removed because later we find Joseph dealing with his family over those episodes in his life. But the pain was gone! His heart was free. He was not emotionally or mentally churned up by memories of what had happened.

For thirteen long years Joseph had been denied personal freedom and power. He had maintained a right attitude and response to every injustice and disappointment. Now however, he was lord of all Egypt and could do as he pleased. Yet not once did Joseph take advantage of his position to get even with those who had mistreated him.

The test of grace in your life is how you behave, not only when you are denied power but when you have it too. Power didn't corrupt Joseph's heart. The reason he never sought to get even, when he eventually had the opportunity to, was because he carried no bitterness with him. Francis Frangipane defines bitterness as *unfulfilled revenge*. This monster did not exist in Joseph. He was walking in forgiveness toward everyone.

Joseph humbly acknowledged the grace of God in this, 'God made me forget', he said. It can be very hard to do this yourself. But when you hand the memories to God in forgiveness he is able to do a miracle of forgetfulness! It is called divine amnesia.

Joseph saw no need to head back to Canaan and force a showdown. He left it in God's hands. If there was to be a change of heart in his brothers it would have to be the result of a work of God. Confrontation will never change a person. People who have wronged us must be handed over to God for him to work on as and when he pleases. Arguing with the unrepentant is a pointless exercise.

Then Asenath and Joseph had a second son, Ephraim. The name comes from a Hebrew word meaning 'twice fruitful.' God was blessing him in Egypt, the place where he had suffered so much. Joseph didn't need to escape the place to get 'twice blessed'. He just needed a dose of divine amnesia and the stream of blessing would open right up.

These two sons of Joseph represent two principles at work in his life; forgetfulness and fruitfulness. It was because he was able to forget the past that he was able to become fruitful in the present. You cannot be fruitful until you let go of hurt, pain and injustice. Bitterness leads to barrenness. Divine forgetfulness leads to divine fruitfulness.

The past confronted

Joseph was exalted and respected. He enjoyed untold wealth, a happy family, and a position second only to Pharaoh, king of Egypt. Most importantly his famine relief plan was working well. Yet despite all this, there was unfinished business hanging around and God was going to act. So fasten your seat belts! We are about to witness the unfolding of the most dramatic chapter of Joseph's life.

> *When Jacob learned that there was grain in Egypt, he said to his sons, 'Why do you just keep looking at each other?' He continued, 'I have heard that there is grain in Egypt. Go down there and buy some for us, so that we may live and not die'.*
>
> GENESIS 42:1-2

There had been no escape for Canaan in this terrible famine which was engulfing the world, but eventually word filtered through that there was food in Egypt. Now old Jacob instructed his sons to get down there urgently and buy grain to keep them alive, while Benjamin his youngest would stay home and keep him company.

The other ten packed and began the five day journey to secure the lives of the entire clan. They had no idea that God was at work to do much more than just feed them. As far as Jacob was concerned Joseph was dead and the ten brothers continued unrepentant over their crimes. But God had other ideas. The way Joseph handled these estranged brothers is an incredible example of how palace people conduct themselves, of how resurrected with Christ, we actually reign with him.

Now Joseph was the governor of the land, the one who sold grain to its entire people. So when Joseph's brothers arrived, they bowed down to him with their faces to the ground. As soon as Joseph saw his brothers, he recognised them, but he pretended to be a stranger and spoke harshly to them. 'Where do you come from?' he asked. 'From the land of Canaan', they replied, 'to buy food'.

Although Joseph recognised his brothers, they did not recognise him. Then he remembered his dreams about them and said to them, 'You are spies! You have come to see where our land is unprotected'.

GENESIS 42:6-9

Imagine Joseph's thoughts as, without warning, the very brothers who had betrayed him suddenly appeared before him! It had now been over twenty years since he had last seen them. It was obvious they had not the slightest recognition of him. Why should they? In their minds he would almost certainly be dead by now. But as he scanned their faces he knew without a doubt it was them. The scripture says, 'he recognised them'.

What would Joseph do? How would he react to this latest twist of destiny? We are going to watch an amazing work as hostile, angry people change before our eyes. We will discover that no one is beyond the reach of God's goodness and we should never exclude anyone from the realms of the grace of God.

For further study

- If you realise you have not yet received Christ as your Lord and saviour, use the prayer below to make your first time commitment to him.

  Heavenly father, I thank you that you love me and sent Jesus to die in my place on the cross, bearing the punishment for my sin in his own body.

  Lord Jesus, I come to you today confessing my sin. I receive you into my life as Lord and saviour. I trust in the sacrifice you made for me.

  I thank you that you rose from the dead and defeated Satan, sin and death once and for all time.

  I pledge my life to you, to be your disciple, to walk in obedience to your word and your will.

  Thank you for hearing me and receiving me today.

  Amen

- The names Joseph gave his two sons revealed that he had dealt with is past. Are you at peace with your past? If there is anything dogging your steps and spoiling your life today, hand it over to God and ask that the blood of Jesus cleanse you from its power.

- Read Ephesians 2:1-10 and spend some time meditating on it. Thank God that you reign in Christ in the heavenly places.

- Now read Genesis 42-45.

CHAPTER 9

Reconciled

We are approaching the climax of an amazing drama; the reconciliation of Joseph and his brothers. Many years had passed but now they stood before him. Then to crown the moment with irony the brothers bowed before Joseph. At that precise moment memories of those long-ago dreams, must have come flooding back. Here they were, just as he had seen, his jealous brothers, hungry and tired, and on their knees before their rejected unrecognisable brother.

How would Joseph, now a ruler in Egypt, respond to this initial encounter? Once again we see his remarkable state of readiness. His words were not those of a man in emotional reaction. He exercised tact and self-control. Joseph began buying time, probing to determine the true state of their hearts and find out vital information about his family.

But they replied, 'Your servants were twelve brothers, the sons of one man, who lives in the land of Canaan.

The youngest is now with our father, and one is no more'.

GENESIS 42:13

Joseph discovered that his beloved Benjamin and his father were alive and well. Now he must work a plan for the reconciliation and salvation of his whole family. He could have used his new found authority to settle scores with his brothers, but he chose not to. Remember, we are going to discover how *palace-people* behave. Joseph is a model for us as believers reigning with Christ. We must dig beneath the surface of the story to see the principles that were operating in his life when dealing with his brothers. Joseph sought no revenge because they were forgiven men. Everything he had been through equipped him to work for the highest motive – their blessing.

Joseph needed to tread carefully though. It was a delicate plan. In order to work there had to be a change of heart in his brothers. So instead of making it easy for them he spoke roughly, accusing them of enemy spying.

As Joseph questioned them, the thing he wanted to know more than anything was the condition of their hearts. He knew he could only be reconciled to his brothers if they were truly repentant. Everything he said and did toward them had this goal in mind. Joseph couldn't give his heart to them unless *their* hearts had changed.

This is where so many people come unstuck in their dealings with others. There is a level of intimacy and openness appropriate to every relationship. You cannot bare your soul to a person unless they are of the same spirit. You cannot open your heart to another person if there is the least suspicion that they are hostile toward you. We must all learn to guard our hearts by setting appropriate boundaries with everyone.

Palace people set boundaries in their relationships

The brothers appeared before Joseph hungry, humbled and guilt-ridden and he served them when he could have killed them! Joseph could see that their consciences had been awakened, but were they yet repentant? Until this was clear he would have to be patient for the process to work its self out. So, having established that his younger brother and his father were safe and well, he puts a test before them:

> *Joseph said to them, 'it is just as I told you: You are spies! And this is how you will be tested: As surely as Pharaoh lives, you will not leave this place unless your youngest brother comes here. Send one of your number to get your brother; the rest of you will be kept in prison so that your words may be tested to see if you are telling the truth. If you are not, then as surely as Pharaoh lives, you are spies'. And he put them all in custody for three days.*
>
> GENESIS 42:14-17

Joseph was turning up the heat! On their release, he makes them a proposition; he'll let most of them go, but keep Simeon as a hostage until they return with young Benjamin. This anguish was more than they could bear:

> *They said to one another, 'Surely we are being punished because of our brother. We saw how distressed he was when he pleaded with us for his life, but we would not listen; that's why this distress has come upon us'. Reuben replied, 'Didn't I tell you not to sin against the boy? But you wouldn't listen. Now we must give an accounting for his blood'. They did not realise that Joseph could*

*understand them, since he was using an interpreter. He
turned away from them and began to weep, then turned
back and spoke to them again.*

GENESIS 42:21-23

How remarkable it is that some 20 years after they had sold
Joseph into slavery his brothers are still plagued by the guilt of
their crimes. It is as if they had just been committed! Now their
consciences were thoroughly awakened and more importantly,
they were taking responsibility for the terrible crime they had
committed all those years ago: 'We saw how distressed he was.'
'We would not listen.' 'We must give an accounting for his
blood.' God was at work in their hearts. They were realising the
gravity of their crime and it was all being made possible because
Joseph was in the palace.

Hearing them speak caused Joseph deep anguish. Genesis
says that he turned away and wept, experiencing both the anguish
of their pain and the joy at what was going on. But as a throne
man he kept his emotions in check. He dare not short-circuit
this delicate process. Now, keeping Simeon in Egypt, Joseph
sends the brothers home with more than they bargained for.

*Joseph gave orders to fill their bags with grain; to put
each man's silver back in his sack, and to give them
provisions for their journey. After this was done for
them, they loaded their grain on their donkeys and left.*

GENESIS 42:25-26

When they stopped for the night they made the troubling
discovery – their money had been returned. Genesis records
that their hearts sank as they turned to each other saying, 'What
is this that God has done?' First their hunger in Canaan then

their experience in the palace had begun to soften their hearts. Now Joseph's kindness became another instrument in the hand of God to bring the brothers to repentance. Just like God, he showed grace to sinners. He was magnanimous when he could have been malicious.

Palace people show magnanimity

It is an awesome thing when you can show grace to people who have abused you or mistreated you. Joseph took no pleasure in seeing the anguish of his brothers. Instead he blessed them. But notice too, that he didn't advertise this fact. The brothers had no idea that the money in the sacks was put there by non other than their wronged brother! It was given discreetly with no strings attached.

Now the brothers were returning home. There was nothing more that Joseph could do at this stage. He must trust God to work the next step through if there was going to be reconciliation.

If Joseph had revealed himself now, he would have by-passed an essential process. He let them go and they returned to their father. To skip this route would have bought a forced reconciliation. The choice would not have been theirs. In releasing them he was giving time for God to work in their hearts and trusting God with the outcome. The love Joseph held for his brothers released them.

Palace people give freedom to others

The love of God is completely liberating. It does not coerce. It never uses guilt or debt to manipulate the desired response. The power of God's love was demonstrated on the cross by an act of supreme sacrifice for an undeserving race. It is amazing and we must be the same in our dealings with others. Loyalty or allegiance gained without freedom is a form of bondage. We must never violate people in such a way.

The second journey

> *Now the famine was still severe in the land. So when they had eaten all the grain they had brought from Egypt, their father said to them, "Go back and buy us a little more food'. But Judah said to him, 'The man warned us solemnly, 'you will not see my face again unless your brother is with you'.*
>
> GENESIS 43:1-3

I believe Joseph knew the brothers would be back and for several reasons. Firstly, they had the famine and he had the food! Hunger brings reality. Secondly, Simeon had been kept by him in Egypt. They could not dismiss the absence of their brother. Finally, Joseph could see that God at work bringing about the long awaited fulfilment of his dreams. He was in the flow of something big!

Joseph waited for the process of repentance to take its effect. The brothers had to humble themselves in order to return for more food. But eventually their father yielded and sent them back with Benjamin and donkeys laden with gifts for the man they all knew as a powerful Egyptian leader.

> *So the men took the gifts and double the amount of silver, and Benjamin also. They hurried down to Egypt and presented themselves to Joseph. When Joseph saw Benjamin with them, he said to the steward of his house,*

*slaughter an animal and prepare dinner; they are to eat
with me at noon.*

GENESIS 43:15-16

This time Joseph lavished kindness on them, wining and dining
them at his home. Imagine the brothers' suspicions at this
unexpected show of hospitality! Was this trickery? Was Joseph
about to take them all as slaves? They thought, 'he wants to
attack us and overpower us and seize us as slaves and take our
donkeys', (Genesis 43:19). As the guilt of past crimes weighed
upon their minds they could only imagine trouble ahead.

Isn't it amazing that while they feared the worst, Joseph
was actually planning the best? Their guilt was colouring their
ability to receive. They were anxious and suspicious. The brothers
approached the steward of the house to explain that after their
first visit they had found their money in the mouth of their
sacks. They continued:

*'So we have brought it back with us. We have also
brought additional silver with us to buy food. We don't
know who put our silver in our sacks.' 'It's alright,' he
said, 'don't be afraid. Your God, the God of your father,
has given you treasure in your sacks; I received your
silver.' Then he brought Simeon out to them.*

GENESIS 43:21-23

The brothers were amazed at these words! What was going on?
They could hardly keep up. One minute they feared for their
lives, the next they were being reassured by this Egyptian that
God had blessed them with the money. What was happening?
The answer is simple; their guilt was being brought to the surface
where they could confront it.

The men were taken to Joseph's house and arrangements made for the midday meal. The Governor arrived and they brought their presents to him. In the intimacy of his own home he was able to take more notice of his brother Benjamin.

> *'Is this your youngest brother, the one you told me about?'*
> *And he said, 'God be gracious to you my son'. Deeply*
> *moved at the sight of his brother, Joseph hurried out*
> *and looked for a place to weep. He went into his private*
> *room and wept there. After he had washed his face, he*
> *came out and, controlling himself, said, 'Serve the food'.*
>
> GENESIS 43:29-31

It was an incredible moment. Joseph, the dignified leader, the deliverer of Egypt, could no longer contain his pent up emotions. He retreated to a private place, the flood gates opened and he wept his heart out! It is comforting to know that there is nothing wrong with emotions and feelings. What Joseph experienced at that point was entirely natural. Reigning with Christ does not rob you of legitimate human emotions. It would be bizarre to say the least, if Joseph had felt nothing deep at that moment!

Palace people express emotions in a righteous way

But such feelings and emotions must be expressed in their appropriate setting. This was not the place for an open display. Joseph ruled his emotions but he did not suppress them! He found a private place and gave vent to what was inside him. These are important lessons. To reign with Christ does not deny our humanity but it does bring it under his rule. Emotions should be acknowledged but not allowed to rule you.

After he had washed his face, he came out and, controlling himself, said, 'Serve the food'. They served him by himself, the brothers by themselves, and the Egyptians who ate with him by themselves, because Egyptians could not eat with Hebrews, for that is detestable to Egyptians.

GENESIS 43:31-32

Joseph returned to the dining room and the meal was served. However, the brothers were about to get another remarkable surprise: they discovered to their amazement that their seating had been arranged in order of their ages, from Reuben down to Benjamin. Someone knew more about them than they had reckoned on. Furthermore, Benjamin was given no less than five times the amount of food as everyone else!

It is a picture of grace! Here were these undeserving guilty men feasting at the royal table. God does not treat people as their sins deserve and neither must we. Joseph lavished kindness on his brothers *before* their reconciliation. The fact that his identity was concealed to them shows us that this was the free expression of his heart.

By now a realisation was dawning on the brothers that a supernatural hand was at work in their lives. It was exposing their guilt and softening their hearts. All the pieces were coming into place for the restoration that God had long been planning.

The road to reconciliation

Reconciliation – what a beautiful word! It speaks of so many wonderful things; forgiveness given and received; restored friendship; healing and peace. It goes so much further than the end of conflict or the opening of dialogue. It is when things are put right; when broken pieces come back together as one.

God had a plan for the reconciliation of Joseph and his family. Painstakingly he brought it to fulfilment and here in Genesis 44 we witness the last remarkable scenes in this epic story.

> *Now Joseph gave these instructions to the steward of his house, 'Fill the men's sacks with as much food as they can carry, and put each man's silver in the mouth of his sack. Then put my cup, the silver one, in the mouth of the youngest one's sack, along with the silver for his grain'. And he did as Joseph said.*
>
> Genesis 44:1-2

Joseph knew that in order to reveal himself he had to be sure of his brother's attitudes: namely their trust toward God and their humility toward man. Joseph arranged for a silver cup to be hidden in Benjamin's sack and his steward was sent after the party to confront them over this. Of course the brothers cooperated in the search in all innocence. Why should they be concerned?

To their horror, the precious item was found in Benjamin's sack. The blood must have drained from their faces as they realised the implications of this discovery. Genesis 44:13 says, 'they tore their clothes'. The brothers were brought back to Egypt in great consternation to face the powerful lord whom they had apparently offended. Here was the final opportunity for their hearts to be tested.

Palace people test the motive before trusting the heart

Joseph was ready for their return. His heart ached to make himself known to his family. But he also knew it could only happen if they were ready too. On entering Joseph's house, Genesis records that the brothers, 'threw themselves to the ground before him.' Judah spoke on behalf of them all:

> *'What can we say? How can we prove our innocence? God has uncovered your servants' guilt. We are now my Lord's slaves – we ourselves and the one who was found to have the cup.'*
>
> GENESIS 44:16

What a remarkable confession! No argument, no self-justification, no wriggling. Judah, the ringleader who so many years ago had wanted his brother dead; Judah, the one who had led them all in lying to their father. The work of repentance is almost complete. But Joseph doesn't even stop there. Despite the agony of seeing his brothers suffer, he has to be sure that every grain of pride and deception has been removed from their hearts.

> *But Joseph said, 'Far be it for me to do such a thing! Only the man who was found to have the cup will become my slave. The rest of you go back to your father in peace'.*
>
> GENESIS 44:17

This was no comfort to Judah and the rest. The pressure was pilling up. Their conscience was now fully awakened. To tell their father that Benjamin had been left behind as a slave was unthinkable. This desperate situation brought home the reality of their wickedness all those years ago to another brother they had condemned into slavery. Now Judah cast himself on Joseph's mercy and pleaded with him in what is surely one of the most poignant speeches in the entire bible.

'Please, my lord, let your servant speak a word to my lord. Do not be angry with your servant, though you are equal to Pharaoh himself. My lord asked his servants, "Do you have a father or a brother?" And we answered, "We have an aged father, and there is a young son born to him in his old age. His brother is dead, and he is the only one of his mother's sons left, and his father loves him".

Then you said to your servants, "Bring him down to me so I can see him for myself". And we said to my lord, "The boy cannot leave his father; if he leaves him, his father will die". But you told your servants, "Unless your youngest brother comes down with you, you will not see my face again". When we went back to your servant my father, we told him what my lord had said.

Then our father said, "Go back and buy a little more food". But we said, "We cannot go down. Only if our youngest brother is with us will we go. We cannot see the man's face unless our youngest brother is with us".

Now then, please let your servant remain here as my Lord's slave in place of the boy, and let the boy return with his brothers. How can I go back to my father if the boy is not with me? No! Do not let me see the misery that would come upon my father.'

GENESIS 44:33-34

This contrite appeal was coming from the lips of Judah, the man who 20 years earlier had proposed that Joseph be killed. It represented a complete turn around in the heart of the brothers. Previously Judah had not cared about his father's suffering. Now he was offering himself as a slave to save his father more pain. This was the moment Joseph had been waiting for. He knew his brothers were fully repentant. They were ready for Joseph to disclose himself and he could bear the agony no longer. We are now given access to one of the most moving moments in the story:

> *Then Joseph could no longer control himself before all the attendants, and he cried out, 'Have everyone leave my presence!' So there was no one present when Joseph made himself known to his brothers. And he wept so loudly that the Egyptians heard him, and Pharaoh's household heard about it.*
>
> *Joseph said to his brothers, 'I am Joseph! Is my father still living?' But his brothers were not able to answer him, because they were terrified at his presence.*
>
> GENESIS 45:1-3

The brothers were utterly speechless. Nothing could have prepared them for this revelation. A thousand thoughts must have flashed through their minds. Was this a trick? How did this man know about their past? No, this was none other than their brother Joseph! But how did he get here? No wonder they were terrified. But Joseph took no advantage of their distress. He reassured them; he helped them through their shock. But most of all he presented his perspective on all that had happened to him.

> *Then Joseph said to his brothers, 'Come close to me'. When they had done so, he said, 'I am your brother Joseph, the one you sold into Egypt! And now do not be distressed and do not be angry with yourselves for selling me here, because it was to save lives that God sent me ahead of you'.*
>
> GENESIS 45:4-5

This wonderful scene was only possible because God had worked in the life of Joseph so deeply. Here was a golden opportunity for revenge. Joseph could have humiliated his brothers and taken personal advantage of their distress and weakness. But instead he comforts and reassures them. The time for reconciliation had come. Joseph offers them the perfect forgiveness that he has already been walking in for so long.

Palace people forgive completely

Joseph completely forgave his brothers! And because he walked in this forgiveness he was able to see everything from God's supreme vantage point.

> 'God sent me ahead of you to preserve for you a remnant on earth and to save your lives by a great deliverance. So then, it was not you who sent me here, but God.'
>
> GENESIS 45:7

From the palace Joseph served his brothers, not simply with grain but with forgiveness, reconciliation and future hope. He led them to full repentance so that they could receive all that could be theirs. This is the true nature of spiritual authority. Because Joseph had learned to serve with a right spirit when he was power-less, he would continue to serve in the same spirit when he was power-full.

The key to everything was Joseph's perspective. He was not controlled by scheming vindictive brothers but by a divine, gracious hand. God had sent him to Egypt! It was this attitude that both sustained him through those long bitter years and now enabled him to completely forgive and receive these same brothers.

'God sent me.' This was the truth he walked in. Joseph behaved with integrity and magnanimity in the palace because he had learned to in the prison. He was faithful when he had nothing, so God knew that he would be faithful when he had everything.

Bringing it all home

There is one simple reason why God permitted so many pages of the bible to be given over to this story of reconciliation. It is the example of forgiveness and grace that we all need so desperately. Personally, I have enjoyed a good life. I have not been abused or mistreated like so many others, but I know a man who has – Joseph; betrayed, enslaved, imprisoned, and forgotten. Yet he trusted God and forgave man in a way that shines out supremely. Joseph's story is told so that you can forgive those who have hurt you. His story is included so that you can understand how the will of God can overwhelm suffering and injustice. He is there so that you see how God can work all things for good in your life.

Etched into the story of Joseph is the greater drama of the cross. There Jesus, the saviour of the world, hung in torment and agony, the innocent son of God dying for a guilty world. But in the heart of Christ we find the same two outstanding characteristics that marked Joseph's life; his unshakable trust in God and his forgiveness toward his brothers.

In the garden Jesus prayed, 'Not my will but thine be done'. He utterly committed his life into the hands of his heavenly father. And from the cross he cried, 'Father, forgive them for they know not what they do'. There was not a speck of anger or bitterness toward his persecutors. Therefore, from the crucible of his suffering, God raised Jesus to the throne of heaven from where he is qualified to administer salvation to a needy world.

Jesus forgave when he hung in weakness and torment. Now as our high priest, he continues to work for our good, representing us before the father. So too, Joseph continued to walk in grace toward his brothers for the remainder of his life. Years later when old Jacob died and the brothers feared that Joseph might turn on them; he re-iterated the words he had spoken when first he revealed himself to them.

> *But Joseph said to them, 'Don't be afraid. Am I in the place of God? You intended to harm me, but God intended it for good to accomplish what is now being done, the saving of many lives. So then, don't be afraid. I will provide for you and your children'. And he reassured them and spoke kindly to them.*
>
> GENESIS 50:19-21

Events had moved at lightening speed. Suddenly, a new landscape presented itself to Joseph, one in which his family were very much a part. But there was still one important character yet to find his place in this finale, old Jacob, the broken father and it is to him we will now turn our attention.

For further study

- Consider the following statements from this chapter; to what degree are they true for you?

    Palace people set boundaries in their relationships.

    Palace people show magnanimity.

    Palace people give freedom to others.

    Palace people express emotions in a righteous way.

    Palace people test the motive before trusting the heart.

    Palace people forgive completely.

- Now consider the people God has allowed to come into your life. They are not always people you would have chosen. Sometimes there are issues that need settling. Pray for those people right now and seek ways to bless them and help them.

- Now read Genesis 46-50.

CHAPTER 10

Jacob Restored

It's no secret that I love the movies! If a film touches me in a special way, I will watch it over and over again. One of my favourite movies of the Eighties was John Boorman's *The Emerald Forest*. Based in fact, it tells the story of Bill Powers, a dam engineer in Brazil whose young son Tomme (played by Charlie Boorman, the director's son) is kidnapped by a rainforest tribe. Bill Powers spends the next ten years desperately searching for his son not knowing if he is alive, but never giving up hope.

Finally, father and son come face to face deep in the jungle. But it isn't just the passage of time that has altered their lives: Tomme has been brought up as a member of an indigenous Amazon tribe. They now belong to different worlds! You can see the unspoken, anguished question in the father's eyes, 'What has happened to my son?'

Jacob must have been just as profoundly shocked upon learning that his son Joseph was alive and of all things, Prime Minister of Egypt. But there is one important difference.

Instead of living in hope like Bill Powers, Jacob had lived in grief and despair, for 22 years convinced that his son was dead. Until now our story has centred almost entirely around the person of Joseph. But, throughout, Jacob has been there in the background, never far away. Now in the closing chapters of Genesis he's back and centre-stage.

Joseph and Jacob

Until now Joseph's energy had been taken up in dealing with the matter in hand – reconciliation with the eleven brothers! But from here on his priorities would change. Having established that his beloved father was alive, he must now consider his welfare. A heavenly plan was already taking shape and God had put it into the mind of Pharaoh: Jacob and his entire household must move to Egypt to ensure their survival for the remainder of the famine.

> *When the news reached Pharaoh's palace that Joseph's brothers had come, Pharaoh and all his officials were pleased. Pharaoh said to Joseph, 'Tell your brothers, "Do this, load your animals and return to the land of Canaan, and bring your father and your families back to me. I will give you the best of the land of Egypt and you can enjoy the fat of the land"'.*
>
> GENESIS 45:16-18

After so many years the spotlight now returns to Jacob. We are going to get inside the heart and mind of this old patriarch and our reintroduction to him provides a powerful reminder of what we have been learning throughout our story. Because sadly, while the son had moved on in the grace of God, the father had not! Jacob's story is a sober lesson in the power of unbelief. But it is also a lesson in the power of grace, because he didn't remain in the place we find him! Despite all his challenges, he finished strong! But first of all, it is important to notice Jacob's reaction to the amazing news the brothers bring him:

> *So they went up out of Egypt and came to their father Jacob in the land of Canaan. They told him, 'Joseph is still alive! In fact he is ruler of all Egypt'. Jacob was stunned; he did not believe them. But when they told him everything Joseph had said to them, and when he saw the carts Joseph had sent to carry him back, the spirit of their father Jacob revived. And Israel said, 'I'm convinced! My son Joseph is still alive. I will go and see him before I die'.*
>
> GENESIS 45:25-28

Such news was the last thing Jacob had expected to hear – and he was shocked. The Amplified Bible puts it like this, 'And Jacob's heart began to stop beating and he almost fainted'. One could be tempted to feel sorry for him, 'Poor old Jacob – we shouldn't be too hard on him. After all his favoured son was snatched away and everything suggested he had been killed'. But the fact is that Jacob had been living all these years in a crippling unbelief that had all but finished him off.

Let's go back in time and remind ourselves of what happened on that fateful day when the eleven brothers returned from the fields with Joseph's tattered robe in their hands:

> *Then they got Joseph's robe, slaughtered a goat and dipped the robe in the blood. They took the ornamented robe back to their father and said, 'We found this. Examine*

> *it so see whether it is your son's robe'. He recognised it*
> *and said, 'It is my son's robe! Some ferocious animal has*
> *devoured him. Joseph has surely been torn to pieces'. Then*
> *Jacob tore his clothes, put on sack-cloth and mourned for*
> *his son many days. All his sons and daughters came to*
> *comfort him, but he refused to be comforted. 'No', he said,*
> *'in mourning will I go down to the grave to my son'. So*
> *his father wept for him.*
>
> GENESIS 37:31-35

All they did was to present the bloodstained tunic and Jacob decided to believe the worst. He didn't pause, not for a moment, to ask God or even quiz his sons concerning their highly unlikely find! He simply accepted what appeared as material evidence. Immediately a dark cloud of grief and anguish descended on Jacob's soul. Genesis tells us that, 'He refused to be comforted'. And that is exactly how he remained.

Now just contrast how quick Jacob was to believe the worst concerning his son with how slow he was to believe the brothers' report that Joseph had been found alive! That is the mark of unbelief – receive the bad report, reject the good report!

The two agents of unbelief are physical evidence and logical thought, our senses and our mind. But neither should be given the power to determine our state of heart. Look at the consequences for Jacob. From that moment he lived in a morbid grief which sucked the very life from him. It could have been so different: by choosing to live in hope he would have seen the hand of God at work and contributed to the process of reconciliation.

If anyone had good reason to indulge in unbelief it was Joseph. He was the one who had been betrayed and sold into Egypt, the one who had suffered injustice and imprisonment.

Joseph was the one whose hopes had been dashed again and again, not Jacob.

Unbelief is a cursed thing. It blinds and cripples its victim. Back and forth went his sons to buy grain in Egypt, yet throughout the entire saga not once did Jacob detect the hand of God at work! If anything, he prolonged the process through his unbelief. Unbelief that had such a strong hold, that his first response to the good news about Joseph was to reject it. It was only, 'when they told him everything and showed him the carts', that his heart softened and he allowed himself to believe the evidence, 'I'm convinced! My son Joseph is still alive. I will go and see him before I die', (Genesis 45:28).

But even then, Jacob is preoccupied with himself. Isn't he glad for Joseph's sake? Doesn't he want to rejoice in the provision of God for his family? Unfortunately the best he can muster is that he can now die in peace! I'm sorry, but this is one selfish old man!

The carnal and the spiritual

Jacob's fundamental problem was carnality. The word 'carnal' means sensual. We tend to think of sensual as meaning sinful, particularly with sexual connotations. But sensual simply means 'ruled by our senses'. Jacob's unbelief was based on physical evidence, on what his senses told him. He was trapped in the world of his senses and logical thoughts. Jacob was a 'carnal believer'. Despite the fact that he had seen and known so much of the invisible world, he was now imprisoned in the visible.

Joseph, on the other hand, was a man dominated by the invisible realm. His faith was based on supernatural evidence and he lived by what he knew of God. He trusted in God above his senses and circumstances.

Bill Johnson has said, 'Unbelief is faith in the visible realm'. That is an apt description of Jacob. He saw the 'evidence' of the bloodstained robe and for 22 years he was trapped by the lie of this evidence. One moment of carnality exacted a terrible price – and it should have been so different! Jacob had a track record of walking with God that Joseph didn't have. He had encountered God supernaturally at Bethel, where he had heard his voice and received awesome promises concerning his own life and that of his offspring.

> *And God said to him. 'I am God almighty; be fruitful and increase in number. A nation will come from you and kings will come from your body. The land I gave to Abraham and Isaac I also give to you, and I will give this land to your descendants after you'.*
>
> GENESIS 35:11

Jacob had seen the providence and grace of God time and again; he had worshipped, prayed, built altars and known the ways of God over many years. He had wrestled with the angel of God and received his blessing:

> *Jacob replied, 'I will not let you go unless you bless me'. The man asked him, 'What is your name?' 'Jacob,' he answered. Then the man said, 'Your name will no longer be Jacob, but Israel, because you have struggled with God and with men and have overcome'. Jacob said, 'Please tell me your name?' But he replied, 'Why do you ask me my name?' Then he blessed him there. So Jacob called the name of the place Peniel, saying, 'It is because I have seen God face to face, and yet my life was spared'.*
>
> GENESIS 32:26-30

He had received dreams, revelations, protection and providence. He had also seen how carnality had robbed his brother Esau of his birthright, but still he allowed years of his own life to be stolen by that same carnality.

Joseph however, was a mere 17 year old lad with nothing but a couple of dreams for security. Yet that was enough to guard his soul through years of injustice. Jacob didn't even detect the hand of God in those dreams when Joseph reported them. They could have been an anchor for his own life, an assurance that God would keep him safe. But he rejected them just as his other sons had.

Then consider how each of these men lived their lives during those two decades; while Joseph spent his time serving others, Jacob lived in morbid self-pity. Joseph served Potiphar, the prison warden, the cupbearer, Pharaoh and finally the world while Jacob spent his energies grieving and sulking. Unbelief is ultimately a selfish state of heart. It is a prison that holds you in self-obsessed living, 'Look what has happened to me. See how awful and unfair my life has been'.

As a consequence, Jacob stopped hearing the voice of his God. The man who had walked with God for so long lost the joy of his heavenly father's voice. It was only when he believed and took action in moving to Egypt that God began speaking to him again.

I have watched countless people grow old over the years. In every case, regardless of what life has thrown at them, I have observed that people either grow bitter or better. It is a choice we each make for ourselves regardless of the hand life has dealt us. Joseph made the right choice from the moment he was betrayed, Jacob did not!

Ruling and reigning with Christ is an opportunity everyone has. Jacob had not learned to rule over his mind or his emotions.

Consequently, when the big challenge came he buckled on the inside. When temptation came knocking on the door everything he had known and experienced of his God before counted for nothing. Just like Jacob, life will lay before us persuasive evidence, 'things are bad, the situation is hopeless, and everything has gone wrong'. Those are the moments we have everything to gain or lose, to decide what and who we will believe.

Jacob restored

Despite all of this aren't you grateful for grace? Where would any of us be if God left us to stew in our failures and foul-ups? Isn't it a sheer relief that, 'God does not treat us as our sins deserve' (Psalm 103:10). I am so thankful that Genesis doesn't finish with Joseph as a success and Jacob left as a failure. Joseph is our model; an inspiring man who overcame the dark challenges of life. But even if you feel more like a Jacob right now; take heart because God is in the business of restoring the Jacobs. He loved him. There were unfulfilled purposes in his life.

This story is about the grace of God shown to the whole family. We have watched how Joseph walked in grace through all his adversity. We have seen how the eleven brothers received grace. Now Jacob was going to experience grace too.

You may be aware that unbelief has stolen things from you. You may have allowed outward evidence or inner thoughts to dictate the course of your life instead of trusting and believing God. The wonderful news is that God has not finished with you yet. All the time that Jacob was trapped in unbelief, God was in control and planning for him in love. It will be the same for you too! God's purposes are bigger than our failures. Don't look to wasted years or indulge in remorse. You can get back into the grace of God without delay.

Now here is a vital lesson in receiving grace and restoration; God reached out to Jacob, but he still had to take a step of faith. He had to believe the report that Joseph was alive:

And Israel said, 'I'm convinced! My son Joseph is still alive. I will go and see him before I die'.

GENESIS 45:28

Although God stretched his hand of mercy toward him, Jacob needed to respond with faith. The way out of grace was through unbelief. The way back into grace is through faith.

Jacob's restoration however, required more than just a new belief. *He must act!* Even with the decision to believe the report of the brothers, Jacob had to commit one hundred percent to act on what he now believed. Restoration is co-operation with the grace of God. If you want to get back into faith it will come by believing *and* changing. That is the only way.

Finally, that act of commitment must be total. Genesis 46:1 says that, 'Israel set out with all that was his'. Jacob took everything with him to Egypt. There were no half measures, no holding back. He burned his boats with God. Once again, he fully embraced God's will for his life.

So Israel set out with all that was his, and when he came to Beersheba, he offered sacrifices to the God of his father Isaac. And God spoke to Israel in a vision at night and said, 'Jacob! Jacob!' 'Here I am', he replied. 'I am the God of your father', he said, 'Do not be afraid to go down to Egypt, for I will make you into a great nation there. I will go down to Egypt with you, and I will

*surely bring you back again. And Joseph's own hand will
close your eyes'.*

No sooner had Jacob began the journey to Egypt, God began moving on his life again. He stopped at Beersheba and offered sacrifices to the Lord. There the heavens were opened on Jacob again and God revealed himself supernaturally. Once you get yourself fully on track again, be assured heaven will open and you will begin to hear the voice of God once more.

Life in Egypt

Despite Jacob's struggles and failures, the important thing is that he finished strong. That's what counts in life. Don't go out on a whimper. Don't join the ranks of the cynics and critics. Complete your days as a pilgrim and pioneer. The final chapter of Jacob's life took place where God intended; living in Egypt, reunited with his son, enjoying God's abundance and ministering God's word. He ended fruitfully.

Jacob's time in Egypt is a picture of life in the grace of God. He was a restored man and he was going to enjoy the goodness of God. He didn't deserve it. He hadn't worked for it, but God was going to lavish it on him anyway. That is the nature of grace.

Firstly, Jacob enjoyed renewed relationships; the family had been re-united. It is an amazing testimony to the grace of God that the brothers chose to live under Joseph in Egypt and that forgiveness had flowed all around. There had been a remarkable work of grace and a change of attitude in their lives. It could have been so different with recriminations flying and a strained coexistence.

Grace enables you to enjoy a renewal of relationships. It is not something you can force. It has to work in time. But once you are walking in faith again, it is amazing how God works in people to break down barriers and restore friendships.

Secondly, all Jacob's needs were taken care of in Egypt. Joseph presented his father and his brothers to Pharaoh and they were given pasture land for their flocks – the best land around in fact!

> *Pharaoh asked the brothers, 'what is you occupation?'*
> *'Your servants are shepherds', they replied to Pharaoh,*
> *'just as our fathers were'. They also said to him, 'We have*
> *come to live here awhile because the famine is severe in*
> *Canaan and your servants' flocks have no pasture. So*
> *now, please let your servants settle in Goshen'. Pharaoh*
> *said to Joseph, 'Your father and your brothers have come*
> *to you; settle your father and your brothers in the best*
> *part of the land. Let them live in Goshen. And if you*
> *know of any among them with special ability, put them*
> *in charge of my own livestock'.*
>
> GENESIS 47:3-6

With the gift of this fertile land from Pharaoh, they didn't just have enough to get by. Grace brought them into abundance. Sadly the church today is still largely uncomfortable with the idea of God blessing us with more than the minimum. We must see however, that the message of biblical prosperity is not for the rich and wealthy. It is for the poor. It is to break the yoke of poverty and raise people up to a place of plenty.

God brought Jacob out of famine and into abundance. And it wasn't to live on handouts in Egypt. The family prospered in their business as shepherds. Grace causes you to prosper through every channel and avenue that the Holy Spirit opens up for you. That is what grace does for you.

Finally, old Jacob found a place of ministry and fruitfulness in Egypt. It was here that he heard the voice of his God once more and flowed in prophecy and blessing. Genesis 48 and 49 contain a record of the blessings this patriarch imparted to each of his sons. As a restored man, he went on to leave a legacy in the lives of others. He didn't finish in bitterness and remorse. He finished giving blessing and prophesying into the future. Grace enables you to minister to others where once you were preoccupied with yourself.

Joseph's bones

Chapter 11 of the book of Hebrews contains a remarkable catalogue of the heroes of faith and of no surprise to us, Joseph is found there too. What comes as a shock, however, is how such an inspiring life is recorded for posterity:

> *By faith Joseph, when his end was near, spoke about the exodus of the Israelites and gave instructions about his bones.*
>
> HEBREWS 11:22

That's it! There is no record of his fulfilled dreams, nothing about his perseverance in suffering or even his famine relief plan. Of all that could be said we find just a passing mention about bones! This comment in Hebrews is in fact drawn directly from the closing words of the book of Genesis:

> *Then Joseph said to his brothers, 'I am about to die. But God will surely come to your aid and take you up out of*

this land to the land he promised on oath to Abraham,
Isaac and Jacob'. And Joseph made the sons of Israel
swear on oath and said, 'God will surely come to your
aid, and then you must carry my bones up from this
place'. And Joseph died at the age of a hundred and ten.
And after they embalmed him, he was placed in a coffin
in Egypt.

GENESIS 50:26

Why is this? Why does the writer to the Hebrews comment on nothing more than Joseph's bones? The reason is that Joseph's faith reached beyond his own life. It extended into the future to embrace events hundreds of years ahead. The presence of his bones along with his instruction was a prophetic statement – the people of God had a future. Their destiny was secure! This is actually the greatest testimony of Joseph's life.

Joseph served the purposes of God not only for his own life but for those who were as yet unborn. The instruction about his bones was a declaration of God's intent for every generation to come. 'We are not staying in Egypt', it was saying, 'we have a future secured by God's word'. That is ultimately what Joseph's whole life was about; serving the will and plan of God that runs like a thread through the pages of history.

When you and I commit our lives to a similar life of faith we serve that same line of purpose. You see, at the end of the day it is not about you and me, our needs being met or our vindication being secured. It is all about him! It is all about Jesus, his fame, his glory and his kingdom coming on earth as it is in heaven.

The book of Genesis began with humankind walking in fellowship with their God. Heaven and earth were united. As we have seen, the events of the fall disfigured and marred

that wonderful situation. But Genesis concludes with the unity
of the human race being restored under the rule of Joseph. In
picture form we are given a glimpse into God's cosmic plan of
redemption: the bringing together of all things under one head
Jesus Christ, the source of salvation. Or, as Paul put it:

> *And he made known to us the mystery of his will
> according to his good pleasure, which he purposed in
> Christ, to be put into effect when the times will have
> reached their fulfilment – to bring all things in heaven
> and on earth together under one head, even Christ.*
>
> EPHESIANS 1:9-10

Ultimately, that divine purpose is fulfilled through a multitude
of ordinary men and women submitted to Jesus Christ and
walking in obedience to his rule of love. It is a love more powerful
than pain, greater than grief, stronger than sin. In Joseph's case
it embraced a mixed-up, dysfunctional family taking them from
failure and sin all the way into abundance and blessing. So it is
with you and me; that same grace overwhelms every misfortune
of life, leads us through every 'house' we dwell in and secures us
in its eternal plan.

For further study

• Are there any areas of unbelief in your life? Are you listening to the voice of reason and senses instead of the Holy Spirit? Confess that to God right now and begin agreeing with him over those things.

• Are you enjoying the grace of God? Don't live in regret or remorse. Thank God for his grace now and determine to get back in the full flow of his will for your life.

• Are there unfulfilled promises remaining over you? Remind yourself about them and commit them to God afresh. Now determine to walk in faith and right attitude for their fulfilment.